Edible Wild Plants of Eastern United States and Canada

by John Tomikel

ALLEGHENY PRESS

This is a modified reprint of the original text published in 1976. Some photos and other material have been added to the original text.

ISBN 178 1515062622   and 1515062627

The original publication was the following:
Library of Congress Catalog Card: 75-25198
ISBN 0-910041-21-7 paper bound
ISBN 0-910042-22-5 cloth bound

The cloth bound copies are rare and expensive.

Cover design was by Sandra King

CONTENTS

consult the index for page numbers of illustrations and text pertaining to a specific species

Shaggy Mane mushroom found on lawns. Prepare them for consumption before they turn inky. See page 92.

1
INTRODUCTION WITH NOTES ON PREPARING THE PLANTS FOR CONSUMPTION

Plants are the bottom rung on the ladder of life and upon which all higher forms in the ecological system are dependent. Humans have utilized all plants in some form or other. Plants have provided humans with food, clothing, housing, bedding, dyes, utensils, esthetics, and animal forage: the list is endless and just the mere mention of some of these easily stresses the point.

This book is concerned with the nutritional aspects of plants and it deals with the more common edible plants found in eastern United States and Canada. In my first book on edible wild plants I stated that it was "not written as a survival manual" and then proceeded to list most all edible species of the area involved. This work differs in that I do not mention all edible species known to me and I omit species which are edible but not worth the effort of gathering and preparation. Such plants as skunk cabbage, jack-in-the-pulpit, and black locust may have edible parts under proper preparation but these are such fringe plants that it is a disservice to the reader to occupy time with them and these along with many others are omitted. So, what will be found in this volume are those plants which I deem to be most tasty and edible and commonly found in the east.

Purpose of This Book

The idea behind this work is to provide a usable illustrated reference which is inexpensive to the wild plant hobbyist. Gathering and eating wild plants is a hobby. I hate to put it in these terms since there is a hard core of people suspicious of the future and presently training for survival and to them this is no humorous matter.

Two groups of nature enthusiasts that receive smiles from the uninitiated are bird watchers and wild plant gatherers. I happen to fall into both categories and the good natured ribbing that I beget is a small price to pay for the bountiful rewards I receive from being a bit closer to nature than my smirking brethern. When I gave my first book to a friend as a gift he stated "I hope you sell a pile of these, then you won't have to eat this stuff anymore."

To me, eating wild plants is a mystical experience and I have to be careful or I may be carried away emotionally. To many of my wild food friends it is a religious experience of the first caliber and they are obviously over the deep end of some form of reality. They argue over the values of organic versus chemical fertilizer, wild plants versus domesticates, and plants versus meats. I have grown the same species of carrot under organic fertilizer and chemical fertilizer conditions and was unable to detect any difference in the taste. I didn't analyze them for nutrition and so this argument is still open and I wish to be excluded from it.

I state that gathering wild plants is a hobby which could be useful if survival conditions exist. For the average person though, it will remain an inexpensive hobby. It is cheaper than most hobbies since special equipment and clothing are not needed. Unless one forages his own backyard it is not as inexpensive as buying commercial vegetables. I once walked six miles to get a piece of ginger root. Was the time spent worth more than commercial ginger? To me it was but to an economist it would probably not be.

There are several ideas on eating wild plants that have been passed on to me over the years. One is that if a wild plant was worthwhile as a food it would be cultivated in fields and gardens. Of course many of our wild plants are domesticates which have escaped and all domesticated plants are descendents of wild varieties. Many domesticates and wild plants are fringe varieties which please only a few palates. If it were up to me the sweet potato would not be commercially grown since I eat the vegetable only about once a year and then under protest. I will have to agree with those who hold that the plant must not have universal appeal if it is not domesticated. However, the few times a year that the wild plant is eaten makes the search for them worthwhile and the senses are pleased for the moment.

Poisonous Plants

In my youth and in my growing age I have been told that such-and-such a plant was poisonous by various persons. I have strived to eat the plants mentioned in this work in one form or another. Those that I did not eat have been crossreferenced thoroughly or eaten by persons known to me. In this respect questionable plants have been eliminated from the work or designated as questionable. Regarding the poisonous plants, I was shocked and surprised when I read in a reputable text that the wild parsnip was poisonous. My boyhood friends and I spent many afternoons pulling up these plants along the cinder railroad embankments and dining on the roots which we called wild carrot. Only after taking botany in college did I learn that it was known as wild parsnip.

If you were asked to name poisonous plants you would probably list dogbane, poison ivy, or water hemlock. You should be naming such plants as tomato, potato, peach, and a host of plants growing around the home. You see, we only eat certain parts of the plants. It is not different in the wild, in many instances only a limited portion of the plant is edible. This book tries to identify those portions. For the more common wild poisonous plants, refer to Section I of this book. Where portions of edible plants are poisonous then these are mentioned where they are listed in the text.

Use of Scientific Names

One cannot entirely rely on common names for identification of plants. Everyone knows what the dandelion looks like, however, other names may be suspect. There are many varieties of plants which are called pigweed, therefore I have used scientific names for all the plants listed. If one is unfamiliar with the wild plant names then he would be wise to have a flower guide, weed guide, or tree guide in his possession when using this book. These can be referenced to the scientific names. The value of scientific names is that only one plant can have the name and the plant cannot be known by any other scientific name. It must be remembered that two names make up the scientific name, for example, *Taraxacum officinale* is the dandelion. Many other plants use the first name or the last name but only the Dandelion uses the complete name. Different forms of dandelions use different last names which is the specific name, the first name is the generic name and identifies closely related species. Hence, in the oak family we have *Quercus alba* the white oak, *Q. montana* the chestnut oak, and *Q. velutina* the black oak. Notice that once the generic name is used and a sequence follows the generic name may be abbreviated. The specific name is never abbreviated.

Proceed Slowly in Eating

In beginning to eat a new variety of wild plant the diner should proceed slowly, perhaps eating a small portion the first time. Then he should be cognizant of his gastric condition. Some plants may have a laxative effect, others may cause stomach gases to build up, others may simply cause heartburn. People who dined with me on wild plants have been known to complain of those symptoms mentioned when the plant had not affected me. My personal major complaint has dealt with aftertaste in such things as nuts and the bitterness of some roots which usually lose their bitterness after boiling. As a general rule, if one is cautious he may throw away the first water of cooked greens, this would eliminate aftertaste and laxative qualities of some plants for most people.

Methods of Preparation

Basically wild plants are prepared for consumption the same as domestic plants. If it resembles spinach then it can be cooked as you would cook spinach, that is providing the plant is edible. Below is a listing of some basic preparations of plant parts. However, you can use these in any recipe that you can use similar domestic plant parts.

Most recipes for wild plants state that the plant should be boiled, drained, buttered, salted, and peppered. This is so universal a method of preparation that shoe leather is made palatable by this system. Get some variety by trying other recipes.

NOTE: This is a general listing applying only to edible plants. Refer to the specific plant in this text for recommended methods of preparation in case there are any.

roots—eat raw, peel and eat raw, boil, roast, deep fry, pulverize and use as floor for breads, roast some species roots and use as a coffee substitute.

stems—eat raw, peel and eat inner parts raw, cook as you would cook asparagus, unless starving, confine yourself to young tender plants.

leaves—use raw as salad greens, cook as spinach greens, use in making tea, in some cases the first and perhaps second boiling water must be discarded when cooking bitter greens.

flowers—use raw in salads, ferment for wine, pickle pods.

twig buds—eat raw or roasted.

fruit—same uses as apple like fruits or single seeded fruits.

seeds—same uses as oats for grass like seeds and nuts for tree seeds.

II
POISONOUS WILD PLANTS

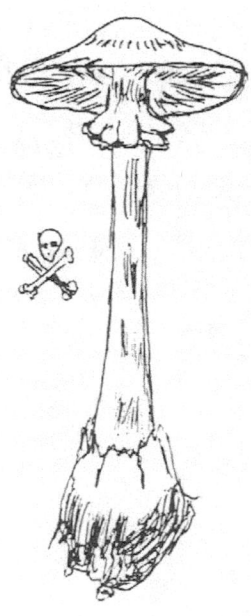

Figure 126

Deadly Amanita

Death Angel mushroom showing the veil around the stem.

The bulb root of the death angel may not always be as pronounced as this.

The veil around the stem and the ghostly color are a good indicators of the death angel. However, there are red and brown varieties of this deadly plant.

Fig. 1 Dogbane
Poisonous

Fig. 2 Jimson Weed
Poisonous

DOGBANE *Apocynum cannabinum* **Figure 1**

The dogbane has a round stem which secretes a milky juice. Its leaves are oblong and its stem forking. Its flowers are bell-shaped. This plant can be separated from milkweed since milkweed does not have forking stems. Dogbane is not fatal to healthy humans but eating it could cause much distress.

JIMSON WEED *Datura stramonium* **Figure 2**

This poisonous plant is coarse and loosely branched and grows to a height of four feet in good soil. Its leaves are large and coarsely toothed. The flowers are white or violet and are borne in the forks of the stem. The fruit is egg shaped and resembles a prickly apple which can be cracked into four parts. It is a native of waste lands, vacant lots, and along roadsides. It loves rubbish heaps. It is poisonous.

POISON HEMLOCK *Conium maculatum* **Figure 3**

This poisonous plant can be mistaken for Queen Anne's Lace

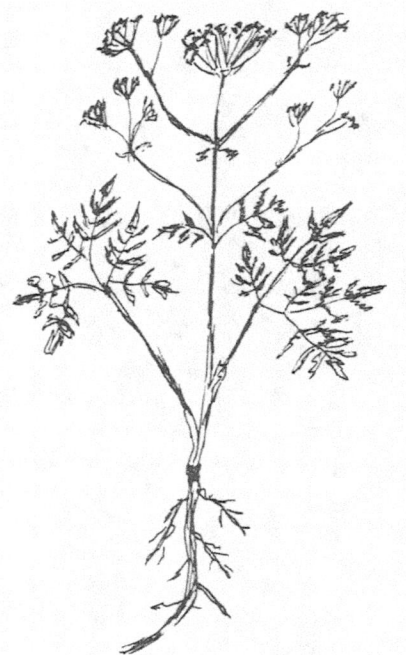

Fig. 3   Poison Hemlock
Poisonous

Fig. 4   Poison Ivy
Poisonous

or wild carrot since it inhabits the same environmental niche. The poison hemlock has a long white taproot which is often branched. Its flowers are in large compound bunches. The flowers are white but do not have the concave or bird's nest nature that is characteristic of Queen Anne's Lace. Approach any carrot like plant with a white flower head with caution.

POISON IVY   *Rhus radicans*   Figure 4

It is surprising how many people are allergic to poison ivy and have had its blisters but have not learned to recognize the plant. The plant appears low and in the grass as an upright plant. It may reach as high as three feet on open land. It also twines around trees and posts and then may reach to fifteen feet. The poison ivy leaves are in groups of three with the middle leaf being longer stemmed than the other two. The poison ivy leaf assumes many shapes and it is difficult to depict accurately for the entire mass of forms it takes. The plant develops white waxy berries. The plant should not be eaten or touched.

WATER HEMLOCK *Cicuta maculata* Figure 5

This poisonous plant appears similar to plants of the carrot family but with much coarser leaves and a thicker and taller stem. The lower leaves are three forked and bear lance shaped or egg shaped toothed leaflets. The stem is smooth, round, and hollow. The white flowers are flat topped and in umbrella like clusters. The root consists of tuber like branches and have a slight parsnip odor. The seeds of the plant are slightly flattened, oblong, and smooth. This plant is extremely dangerous and the eating of it usually ends in death. POISON

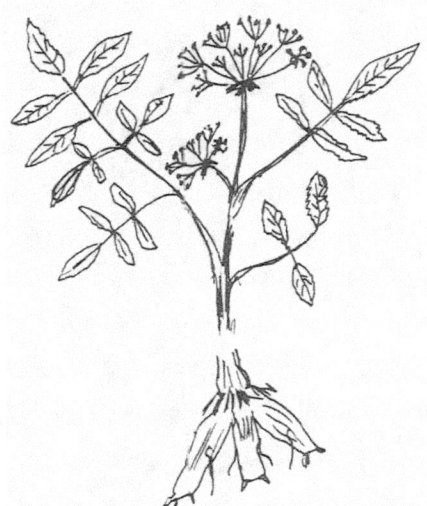

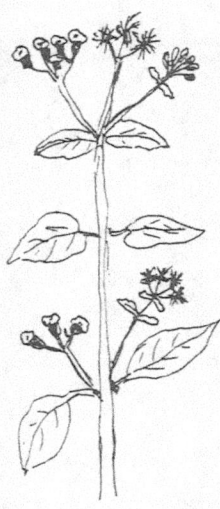

Fig. 5 Water Hemlock
Poisonous

Fig. 6 White Snakeroot
Poisonous

WHITE SNAKEROOT   Figure 6
Eupatorium rugosum   E. urticaefolium

This poisonous plant grows three to four feet tall and has opposite, oval leaves which are coarsely toothed. The plant branches upward and has white flower heads which are small but numerous in flat groups. It is found in woodlands and sometimes in meadows. Cows which eat the snakeroot can transmit this poison by way of its milk to humans. It is alleged that Abe Lincoln's mother died from drinking milk from a cow that had eaten white snakeroot.

III
EDIBLE WATER PLANTS

Spatterdock or Yellow Water Lily   see page 23

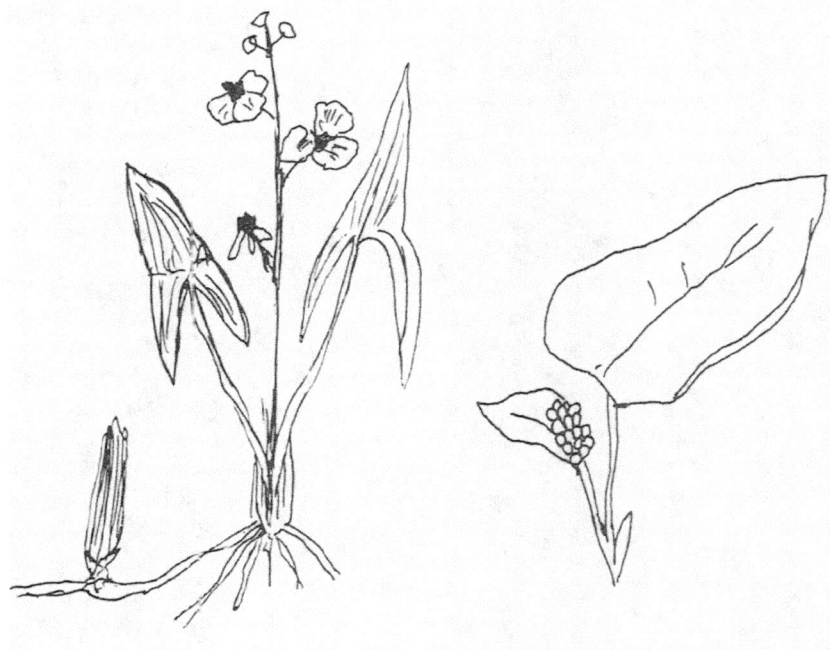

Fig. 7 Arrowhead   Fig. 8 Calla

ARROWHEAD   *Sagittaria latifolia*   **Figure 7**
This aquatic plant grows in shallow water. There is much varia-
tion in leaf size and form. The flower is white and about an
inch in diameter. The tuberous roots are edible raw but are
best boiled and seasoned or roasted on a good hot ash fire. Other
names for the plant are arrowleaf, wapatoo, and Tule Potato.

CALLA   *Calla palustris*   **Figure 8**
The wild calla, also known as Water Arum, is a native of northern
bogs and swamps. It is usually found in black muck but can
be found in other shallow water areas. It has heart shaped leaves
on long stems. The flowers form a mass of greenish white which
turn to red berries late in the season. The root may be gathered,
pulverized, and used as a bread. The user will have to experiment
with this by boiling to suit his own taste.

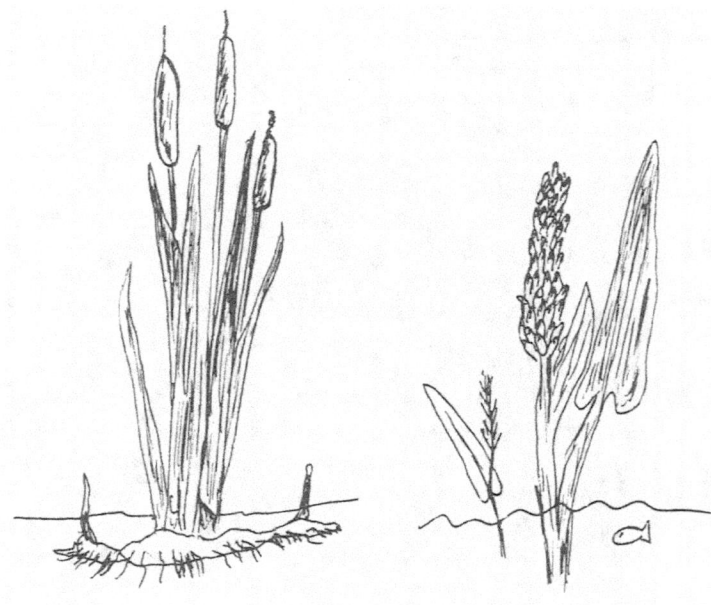

Fig. 9 Cattail   Fig. 10 Pickerel Weed

CATTAIL   *Typha latifolia*   **Figure 9**

This is the tallplant with erect, stiff, reedlike leaves. The root is creeping and branching. The flowers are in dense terminal spikes which finally turn to resemble cotton which shrivels after shedding the pollen. It is a plant of the swamp or wet spot, it is found along the borders of streams and ponds. Almost everything about it is edible. The roots may be peeled and eaten raw or cooked, the greens may be eaten raw or cooked, the flower heads which resemble hot dogs and the pollen they contain may be eaten raw or cooked. The pollen may be used to thicken soups and most parts of the plant may be pickled or used to make jellies. The small cattail, *Typha angustifolia* may be used in a similar manner.

PICKEREL WEED   *Pontederia cordata*   **Figure 10**

The aquatic pickerel weed is narrower and sturdier looking than the arrowhead which it resembles. Its flowers are violet to purple blue and grow into a spike. The nut like seeds can be used for bread or as a cereal.

SPATTERDOCK   *Nuphar variegatum*   **Figure 11**

This yellow waterlily has oval or rounded leaves with a heart shaped base. The leaves may be found floating or erect. The flowers are globes of golden thick petals encasing a round knob of seeds. The plant is found on muddy shores or in shallow water. The large rootstocks may be used as a starchy vegetable, the seeds may be used in breads, soups, or popped like corn. The strong flavor of the root may be removed by twice boiling.

WATER LOTUS   *Nelumbo lutea*   **Figure 12**

This is the largest of the water lily types. It is also known as American water lotus and water chinquapin. Its leaves can get as large as two feet across and these are often raised above the water surface. The flowers are pale yellow and form a flat topped fruit with large nutlike seeds peering from holes. The tuberous roots are edible and make excellent breads. The new

Fig. 11 Spatterdock   Fig. 12 Water Lotus

Fig. 13   White Water Lily

leaves may be used as greens. The large seeds are best used in a half ripe condition. When fully ripe the seeds must be cracked before being roasted or boiled. When dried they can be ground and used in making bread. Do not collect this plant unless there is an abundance.

WHITE
WATER LILY   *Nymphaea ampla*   **Figure 13**

This white water lily has many small petals which grow to two inches in length. The edible parts are the seeds and the tuberous roots which bear round or oval shaped masses which are easily broken off for collecting.

IV
EDIBLE SHRUBS AND TREES

BLACKBERRY

APPLES

There are so many different kinds of wild apples that to classify them on the basis of species is an improbable task. Since I was criticized for leaving this out of my first book I mention it in passing here. To make applesauce, take the apples, slice and simmer them in a small amount of water until tender. Press the apples through a coarse sieve or grind or chop them up until the desired texture is reached. Sweeten to taste. Reheat the sauce until it boils and then pack hot into jars; process as you would other canned goods. For immediate eating just reheat until the desired temperature is reached and/or serve cold.

ASH   *Pyrus and Sorbus species*

The mountain ash resembles a cross between a sumach and a walnut tree. It is found in mountainous country or hill regions. The fruit is a large red cluster of berries which can be used for making jelly, dried and used for making bread, or crushed and steeped for making tea. The berries may be eaten raw but are palatable only when mushy ripe.

BARBERRY   *Berberis canadensis*   Figure 14

This prickly plant is found along fence rows, in rocky pastures, and near wood borders. The leaves are about an inch and a

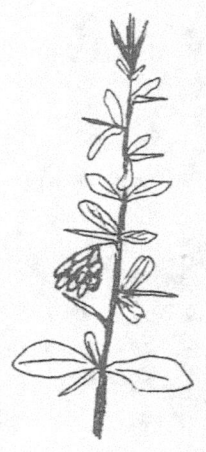

Fig. 14   Barberry

27

half long, and are rounded at the tip and taper toward the base and are sawtoothed. The flowers are pale yellow and droop. The plant is thorny. Its berries are orange red when ripe. Use the berries cooked, in pies, in jellies or eat them raw. The young leaves are also edible. The sap of the wood can be used for a yellow dye.

BEECH   *Fagus grandifolia*   **Figure 15**
The American Beech has long sharp toothed leather leaves, the leaves are yellow green with silky hairs below. The edible buds are red brown and pointed. Beech bark is smooth and never furrowed and the fruit is a brown shiny nut of triangular shape. There are usually two nuts enclosed in a stalked prickly bur which splits when ripe. The beech is found in woodlands and matures to a large tree. The nuts are delicious.

BIRCH

SWEET BIRCH   *Betula lenta*   **Figure 16**
The sweet birch is also known as black birch. The inner bark of this tree has the odor of wintergreen. Its catkins are about three inches long. The leaves are heart shaped at the base and pointed at the apex. The sap may be made into various brews such as wine, vinegar, birch beer, and syrup. The young twigs may be used to make tea. The bark from the roots can also

Fig. 15 Beech

be used for tea. The inner bark makes a good flour when dried and pulverized.

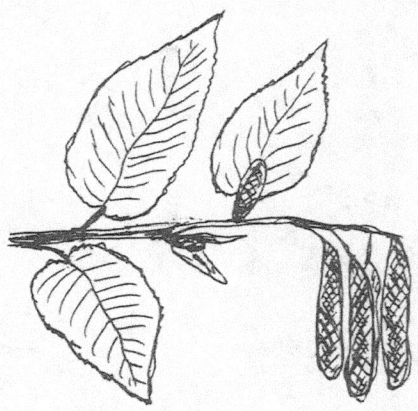

Fig. 16   Sweet or Black Birch

Making Birch Beer

Add 3-1/2 pints of molasses to 7 quarts of boiling water, mix thoroughly and allow to cool for about three hours. To this add a mixture of about 1/2 pound of crushed black birch bark and sassafras bark or root. Mix these and add a half teaspoon beer yeast or baker's yeast, mix again and add four gallons of water. Allow this to ferment for three to four days if you want an alcoholic beverage and only one day for a mild beer. Keep the three day beer away from children. Once you get the hang of it you can experiment with other wild flavorings. Instead of water, birch sap, which is almost water can be used for a stronger flavor.

WHITE BIRCH   *Betula alba*

The white birch is also known as paper birch. Like the sweet birch its inner bark may be used as a flour, it's excellent when mixed with regular wheat flour. The leaves can be used to make tea, and an interesting wine may be made from the sap.

BERRIES

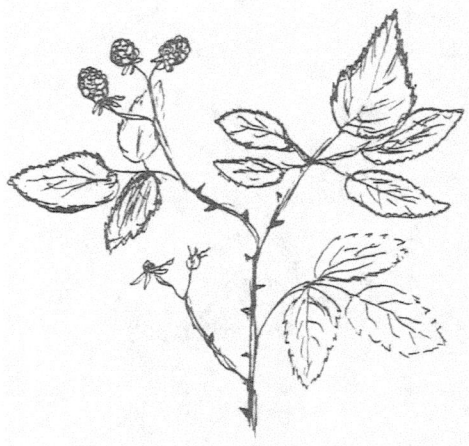 

Fig. 17   Blackberry   Fig. 18   Flowering Raspberry

BLACKBERRIES   *Rubus various species*   **Figure 17**
There are many varieties of blackberries, three of which are
listed here. Uses of blackberries are many and well known. The
mountain blackberry, *Rubus allegheniensis*, grows to seven feet
tall. Older stems are reddish and have very piercing thorns.
Leaves are in clusters of fives or threes and are hairy below.
The tall blackberry, *Rubus villosus* can grow to nine feet. It
usually has three ovate leaves, downy underneath. The dewberry
or running blackberry, *Rubus canadensis*, has trailing stems
and are found at the ground level in thick thorny mats. The
dewberry does not seem as desirable as the higher blackberries.
The dewberry is also classified as *Rubus procumbens*.

BLACKBERRY JAM

Take 8 cups of cleaned berries, combine with 5 cups of sugar
and cook, while stirring occasionally, until the boiling point has
been reached and the sugar dissolved. Then cook until it thickens
to a jell, place in jars and seal with lids or wax.

RASPBERRIES   *Rubus various species*   Figure 18

Raspberries are flattened and mature earlier in the summer than blackberries. Their stems are usually greenish white and have small thorns. The flowering raspberry, *Rubus odoratus*, does not have thorns but sticky hairs which are sometimes like bristles. Its fruit is red. The leaves are large and are usually three to five lobed. The red raspberry, *Rubus strigosus*, has numerous bristles and scattered thorns. The black raspberry, *Rubus occidentalis*, reaches eight feet in length. The leaves are usually in groups of three. This is the most common raspberry and the most desired.

BLACK
CURRANT   *Ribes americanum or R. floridum*

The black currant has smooth branches and smooth berries in long drooping clusters. The shrub is three to five feet tall with leaves which are three to five lobed. The flowers which are greenish white are bell shaped and appear in late April or early May. The currant may be eaten directly or made into pies or jellies.

BLACK HAW   *Viburnum prunifolium*   Figure 19

The black haw is a large shrub, almost a tree with leaves about an inch and a half long with a narrow base. The flowers are in white clusters. The fruit which resembles a small apple like bud is bluish black when ripe. The condition of the fruit varies with growing conditions. When a good bush is discovered one may dine regally from it over a period of many years. Although the black haws may be cooked they are at their best when eaten raw.

BLACK
HUCKLEBERRY   *Gaylussacia resinosa*

The black huckleberry or whortleberry grows to about three feet high and resembles blueberries. It is classed in a different genus due to its different characteristics of flower and fruit arrangements. Leaves of the black huckleberry are oval to oblong. Flowers are reddish. The fruit is shiny black and each contains ten tiny seeds which makes this less desirable than

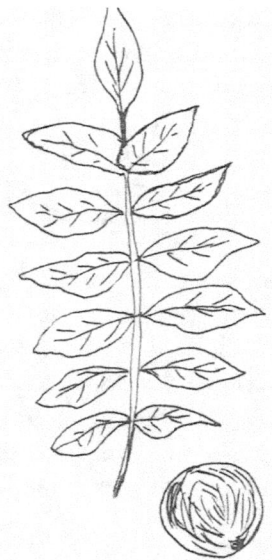

Fig. 19   Black Haw   Fig. 20   Black Walnut

the blueberries. However, the huckleberry is worth searching
out.

BLACK WALNUT   *Juglans nigra*   **Figure 20**
The valuable wood of the black walnut seems to be spelling
its demise. The tree is easily recognized and is presently found
along roadsides and fence rows. The nut is hard to crack and
is taken from its shell with difficulty. The husk juice which
stains ones hands and clothing can be used for dyeing. The kernel
is excellent in cookies.

BLUEBERRY   *Vaccinium species*   **Figure 21**
The blueberry is familiar to every pie lover. There are about
a dozen species of blueberries. They are all edible and confusion
with other berry types is most difficult. The high bush blueberry
grows to fifteen feet. It is also known as swamp blueberry,
Vaccinium corymbosum. The berries are almost black. The low
bush blueberry, *V. pennsylvanicum* grows to a height of about

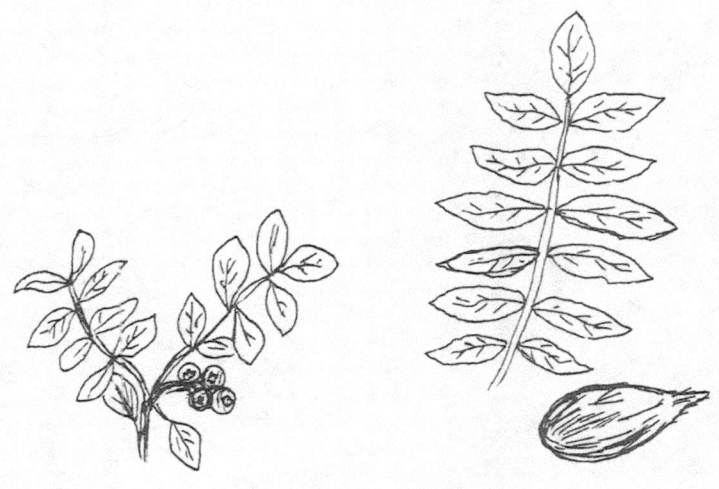

Fig. 21 Blueberry   Fig. 22 Butternut

two feet. The late low blueberry, *V. vacillans* grows to a height of three feet and to my experience is the most common of those mentioned. It is more blue than the others and sweeter. However the berries are smaller in size.

BUTTERNUT   *Juglans cinerea*   **Figure 22**
The butternut seems to be rarer than the black walnut and as the years go by seems to be in existence only by accident. It is difficult to find the trees in deep woods and it seems to be the most abundant in back yards. At one time the butternut was a staple of the early Indian diet. The long nut has a sweet oily flavor much milder than the walnut. The deeply furrowed nut is covered by a thin husk. There is no need to dwell on this delicacy but it is mentioned here to remind the reader that it does exist.

CHERRY

WILD
BLACK CHERRY   *Prunus serotina*   **Figure 23**
The leaves of the black wild cherry are narrow with a tapering tip, they are shiny above and dull below. The twigs and leaves

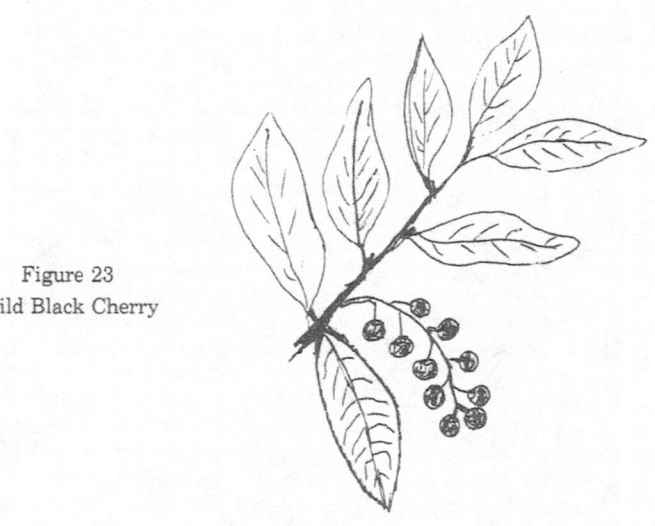

Figure 23
Wild Black Cherry

are bitter when chewed. The black cherry is a large tree. Its flowers are white and hang in clusters. The black to purple fruit is edible and a favorite among winemakers. This tree is much in demand for lumber.

WILD
RED CHERRY   *Prunus pennsylvanica*

The wild red cherry is also known as fire cherry. It has fruits borne in loose tufts along the small branches. It is very sour and has a thin pulp. It is not worth seeking but it is edible. It is great in jellies.

CHOKE CHERRY   *Prunus virginiana*

The choke cherry is similar to the wild black cherry and it takes a concerned individual to tell them apart. The choke cherry is more of a shrub than a tree. The fruit is redder than black. The choke cherry leaves are more oval shaped than the wild black cherry. All three cherries listed have an astringent quality to them.

CRAB
APPLE   *Pyrus angustifolia and P. coronaria*

The crab apples are greenish yellow and very sour. They are best used in preserves and pickled with other fruits. Two types occur in overgrown fields and on the edges of woods. The narrow leaved Crab Apple, *Pyrus angustifolia*, grows to a height of about twenty feet. Its leaves are narrow and glassy and its twigs usually have large thorns. It produces pinkish blossoms in the spring. The American Crab Apple, *Pyrus coronaria*, gets a little larger and it too contains thorns. Its leaves are sharply toothed and often lobed. Its blossoms are rose colored and sweetly scented. These are the fruits which can be put on sticks and whipped across the countryside.

CRANBERRY

The high bush cranberry, Viburnum opulus, has gray brown bark and three lobed leaves which resemble a maple tree. It gets a flat topped cluster of large red berries in late summer. The berries are hard but soften after the first frost. The taste is strongly acid and the berries are best used in jellies or other cooked recipes. Each berry contains a large flat seed. It is from this tree that the Snowball tree of lawn and garden was developed. Refer to figure 24.

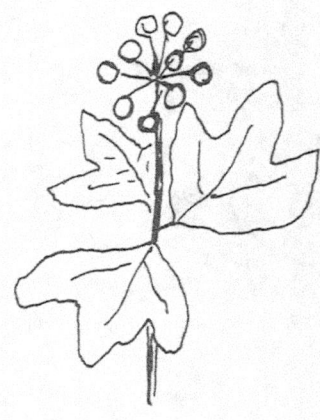

Fig. 24   High Bush Cranberry

The low cranberry, Vaccinium macrocarpon, has slender creeping vines growing to two feet in length. Its leaves are evergreen and its flower is pinkish. The fruit is green and turns red in early fall. The berries are best stewed with sugar. They are not palatable in the raw state.

ELDERBERRY   *Sambucus canadensis*   Figure 25

The elderberry can grow to a height of twelve feet in our area. It has pithy upright stems which are excellent for making choke cherry shooters and whistles. Young stems have green bark which eventually turns gray brown. The flower clusters are flat and pie shaped. The berries are purple when ripe and are excellent raw or in pies and jams. The flowers as well as the fruit can be used to make wine. The flower buds are edible and are good pickled.

ELDERBERRY JELLY

For a small batch take 2 quarts of mostly ripe elderberries, stem and wash thoroughly, then place them in a kettle along with 3 cups of water, bring to a boil. Once boiling, reduce the heat and cook for forty minutes with occasional stirring. Strain the resulting juice through a cloth with as little shaking as possible, discard the berries. Add one and a half cups of fine sugar to each cup of juice and bring to a boil over high heat.

Fig. 25 Elderberry   Fig. 26 Fox Grape

Once the sugar has dissolved pour into clean glasses and seal with melted jelly wax or paraffin. Don't cook much further than enough to dissolve the sugar.

ELM   *Ulmus fulva*
The slippery elm tree can still be found in abundance in our woods despite the Dutch elm disease. The inner bark of the tree can be dried, pulverized, and ground into flour. The inner bark can be chewed upon raw just for curiosity but one would hardly dine on it in that condition.

GOOSEBERRY   *Ribes cynosbati*
It is a joy to discover wild gooseberry plants since they seem to be getting rarer. It is a low shrub with long drooping branches. The leaves are lobed and are usually in clusters of threes or fours with a thorn near the base of each cluster. In the spring the flowers are in groups of three, greenish white in color. The berries are brown red or brown purple when ripe. They are covered with thorny growths but may occasionally be found smooth. Watch out for the berry spikes when eating.

GRAPE   *Vitis species*   Figure 26
In my youth there was always a rumor that wild grapes were not edible. To my present knowledge they are all edible but sometimes not desirable. They are excellent for wine, in preserves, in jellies, and dried like raisens. The summer grape, *Vitis aestivalis* has lobed leaves with short broad lobes that are rusty woolly underneath. The grapes are small and bluish black. The winter grape, *V. cordifolia* and *V. bicolor,* has leaves which are bluish underneath. The fox grape, *V. labrusca,* has leaves which are opposite tendrils or blossom clusters. It too has rusty wool underneath its leaves. The grapes are large and brownish purple in color. The muscadine, *V. rotundifolia,* is recognized by its unbranched tendrils. Its leaves are small with large blunt teeth. The grapes are in small clusters but each grape is large with thick tough skins. Wild grapes like domestic grapes have good and bad years.

WILD GRAPE WINE
Gather a sizable amount of ripe wild grapes. Wash and pick

these clean. Put them into a crock or plastic garbage pail and crush the fruit thoroughly. Add about half as much water as you have fruit juice. Have one teaspoon of wine yeast for each five gallons of batch. You can use ordinary bread yeast for this purpose but a cloudy wine will result. Mix the yeast in a small amount of warm water to get a soupy mess, leave this stand for about a half hour until it becomes frothy and then add this yeast smear to your batch. Wait about four hours and then add about two pounds of sugar for each batch gallon for a dry wine and four pounds of sugar for each batch gallon if you wish a sweet wine. Let this ferment somewhere at a temperature of about 70° F. or room temperature. Cover the batch with a clean cloth. Stir this twice each day until the day the bubbles on top of the wine disappears. When this happens (no longer than the fourth day) transfer the wine into another container by siphoning off the liquid and leaving behind the dregs. You can put it into gallon jugs at this stage. Don't siphon too close to the bottom. It's a shame to waste the bottom wine but this prevents unsightly things from floating around in your finished wine. Fill your jugs to the top leaving just enough room for a cork. Drill a hole in the cork, or purchase one predrilled, and fit it tightly in place, fit it with a piece of plastic tube. Place the other end of the tube in a jar of water, bubbles should appear in the water, if they don't then seal your cork with wax. Bubbles indicate that the fermentation process is still working. Make sure the out end of the hose is in water at all times. You can eliminate the water jar by making a gooseneck in the hose and filling the gooseneck trap with water. When the bubbling stops, the wine is ready. Siphon out the wine and pack into your bottles. Corks are the best stopper. Disturb the batch as little as possible while siphoning. Place the wine in a dark cool place. Wait about a month before trying. The longer you keep the wine the better the quality. Your first batch should be consumed within the first year to see if you did it right. This same recipe can be used for blackberries, choke cherries, elderberries, etc.

GREENBRIER   *Smilax rotundifolia*   Figure 27

The greenbrier is a trailing vine hanging over limbs in the woods. It makes traveling through the woods difficult for it seems to string itself over trails. It develops a cluster of blue black berries

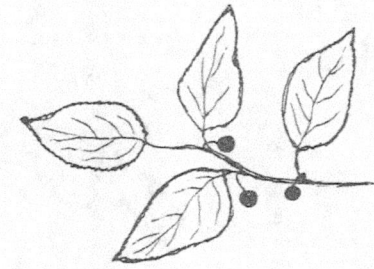

Fig. 27   Greenbrier

Fig. 28   Hackberry

in the fall. The roots may be ground into a meal or used in soups. The new growth may be snapped off and eaten raw or cooked.

HACKBERRY   *Celtis occidentalis*   Figure 28

The hackberry is found on hillsides of new woods. The leaves resemble the elm, pointed and saw toothed. The bark is rough and looks like hard cork. The flowers are small and greenish and are found where leaf stems join the twig. The fruit is brown to purple in color and contains a large seed. Some fruits are pulpy and some are mostly seed. Both extremes are pleasant to eat raw.

HAWTHORN   *Crataegus species*

The hawthorns are small trees with lobed leaves and sharp thorns upon the twigs and limbs. They bear white flowers in the spring which occur in clusters as the ripened fruit does in the fall. The ripe fruit contains hard small seeds and are from red to yellow in color. They resemble little apples. These can be eaten raw or used in making jellies and jams.

HAZELNUT   *Corylus americana, C. rostrata*   Figure 29

The hazelnut bush appears as a clump of twigs, branches, and leaves in a hump up to six feet high. Young shoots are covered

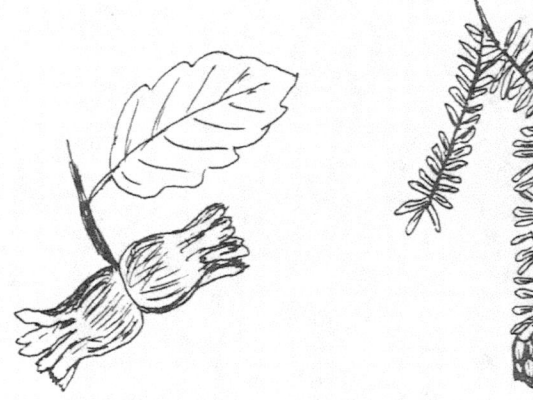

Fig. 29 Hazelnut   Fig. 30 Hemlock

with thin hairs. The leaves are rounded at the base, sawtoothed and sharp pointed. The blooms hang down in catkins. The plant is more common than most people suspect. The beaked hazelnut, *Corylus rostrata*, is a close relative. It is less hairy and grows in smaller clumps. The husk covering the nut is elongated at the tip, hence its name. When ripe, hazelnuts are sometimes thrown clear of the husk and can be collected at the base of the bush. They are good eating raw or in candies.

HEMLOCK   *Tsuga canadensis*   Figure 30

The hemlock or eastern hemlock is a small needled evergreen with needles occurring singly and appearing spirally arranged on the twigs. The needles are dark green above and light green below. The seed bearing cones are less than an inch long, egg shaped, and remain attached all winter. It is a tree of the woodland. Its inner bark can be eaten raw or cooked. The needles may be used to make a tea. Do not consume parts of small plants since this may be confused with the American Yew which is inedible except for its berry. See also Yew.

HICKORY   *Carya species*   Figure 31

The hickory is a well known tree with a nut which varies in size and taste according to species and growing conditions. While burning, the wood has a pleasant odor. The husk covering the

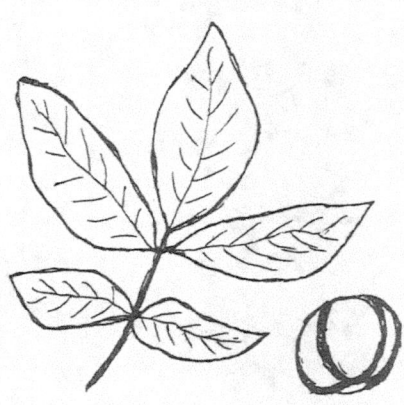

Fig. 31   Hickory

nut splits into four sections yielding a clean nut. The kernel is small and tasty in the shagbark which gets its name from the loose shaggy appearance of its bark, sometimes it is also referred to as shellbark hickory. Hickory leaves are usually in groups of five. The nut of the shagbark hickory, *C. ovata*, the shellbark hickory, *C. laciniosa*, and the mockernut hickory, *C. tomentosa* are sweet or acceptably sweet. The nut of the pignut hickory, *C. glabra* and the bitternut hickory, *C. cordiformis*, are very bitter with a strong aftertaste.

JUNIPER   *Juniperus virginiana*

The eastern red cedar or juniper berries are edible in small quantities. It is the major flavoring in gin. The tree grows in open woods. It is an evergreen with two types of twigs, often on the same tree. Young twigs are sharply pointed while older twigs which bear the fruit are often scaly. The fruit is a bluish berry covered with a whitish powder and has a resinous quality about it.

LABRADOR TEA   *Ledum groenlandicum*   **Figure 32**

This plant which is also known as bog tea is a low growing evergreen which reaches a height of about three feet. Its leaves which alternate are one to three inches long and have rolled outer margins. The leaves are wooly brown underneath. They

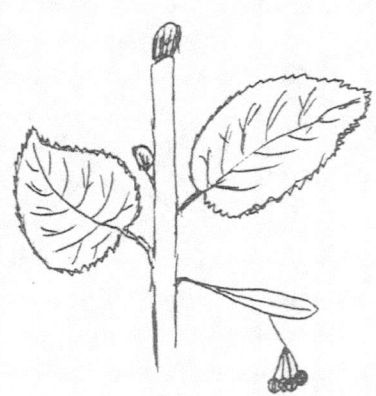

Fig. 32   Labrador Tea   Fig. 33   Linden

are fragrant when crushed. The plant is a native of the cool north and the highlands of the middle states. To make tea, dry the leaves, steep in water, add sugar and lemon if you wish the flavor complimented.

LINDEN   *Tilia americana*   **Figure 33**

The leaves of the linden are heart shaped, shiny dark green on top and smooth duller green below. The margins of the leaves are sharply toothed. Fruit is borne in groups on a long stem and are about the size of a pea. The fruit is attached to a blade or bract. It is a tree of the woodland and is also common along fence rows. The sap of the tree contains a high sugar content and it can be used to make candy. The fruit can be eaten raw in moderation and the flowers can be used to make tea. The buds can also be eaten. The linden is also known as basswood.

LOCUST (HONEY)   *Gleditsia triacanthos*   **Figure 34**

The honey locust is a larger tree than the black locust. As a small tree the honey locust has smooth bark which is colored

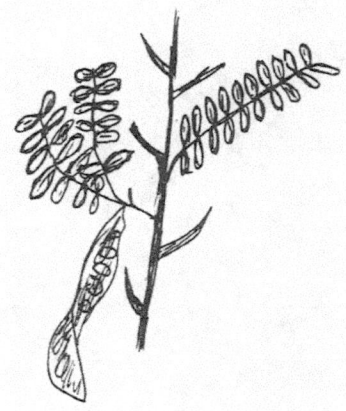

Fig. 34 Honey Locust

in light tones of tan or gray. The trunk of old trees have branching thorns about them. The thorns are modified branches. The leaf stems bear numerous leaflets and the flowers which are greenish white hang in clusters. The seed pods are larger than the black locust and are usually twisted several times. The pods are from ten to eighteen inches long. The pulp surrounding the seed is sweet and may be eaten directly. The seeds are also edible and are best boiled and seasoned. A good beer may be made by fermenting the pods.

MAPLE	*Acer species*	Figure 35

There are many varieties of maple and all of them may be used for making maple syrup, candy, and sugar. The most desirable maple for this purpose is the sugar maple, A. *saccharum*, which has a five lobed leaf with few margin teeth; second in line is probably the silver maple, A. *saccharinum*, which has a five lobed leaf also but with very deep spaces between the lobes. Another common tree is the red maple, A. *rubrum* which has three lobes. The Norway maple, A. *platanoides*, has five lobed leaves but oozes a milky sap when the leaf stem is broken. The Norway maple is the most used for street and commercial tree planting.

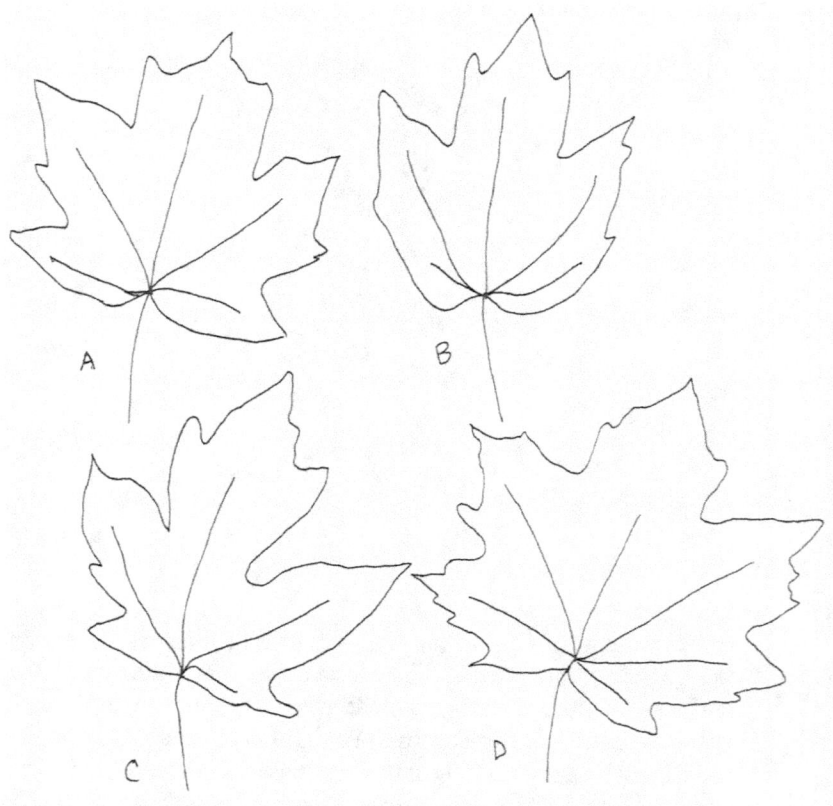

Fig. 35 Maple

A. Sugar Maple   B. Red Maple
C. Silver Maple   D. Norway Maple

MULBERRY   *Morus rubra*   **Figure 36**

This is the berry tree which grows to a height of forty to fifty feet. The leaves are coarse toothed and may be lobed or without lobes. The bark is gray to red brown. The flowers are green and are in spikes or catkins. The edible berry resembles a blackberry, some reaching an inch in length. When edible the berry is red changing to purple. It is sweetest when purple and may be used in pies, jellies, or eaten raw. The white mulberry, Morus alba, is similar to the red in tree habit and growth. Its berries are plumper but have little flavor.

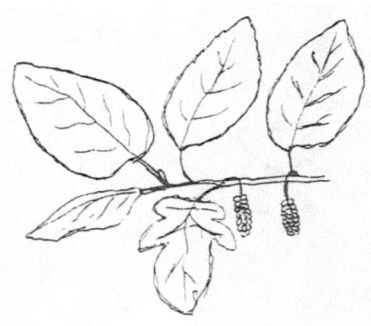

Fig. 36 Mulberry

OAK   *Quercus species*   Figure 37

The acorns of the oak trees are edible, the white oak, *Quercus alba*, is preferred, the chestnut oak, *Q. montana*, is not bad, and the rest are not too acceptable. The scarlet oak, *Q. coccinea*, has bitter acorns and a second boiling is in order before they are palatable. Acorns may be boiled or roasted, they can be ground into meal for bread making. I am under the impression that the rounded leaved oaks produce palatable acorns and the pointed leaved oaks do not, I may be in error there but check for yourself.

PAWPAW   *Asimina triloba*   Figure 38

The leaves of this tree are simple and drooping, they are dark green above and light green below. The fruit which is edible appears as a short stubby banana. It contains numerous brown shiny seeds imbedded in a fragrant outer pulp. The flower which generates the fruit is brownish green and appears before the leaves are out. The fruit is edible raw or cooked. If fallen green fruit is found, it may be kept to ripen.

PEAR   *Pyrus communis*   Figure 39

The wild pear is a variety sprung from the cultivated pear which has escaped to the woods. The wild pear fruit is more round than the tame and its branches are usually thorny. The wild pear is ripe in early September. The quality of the fruit apparently varies with growing conditions.

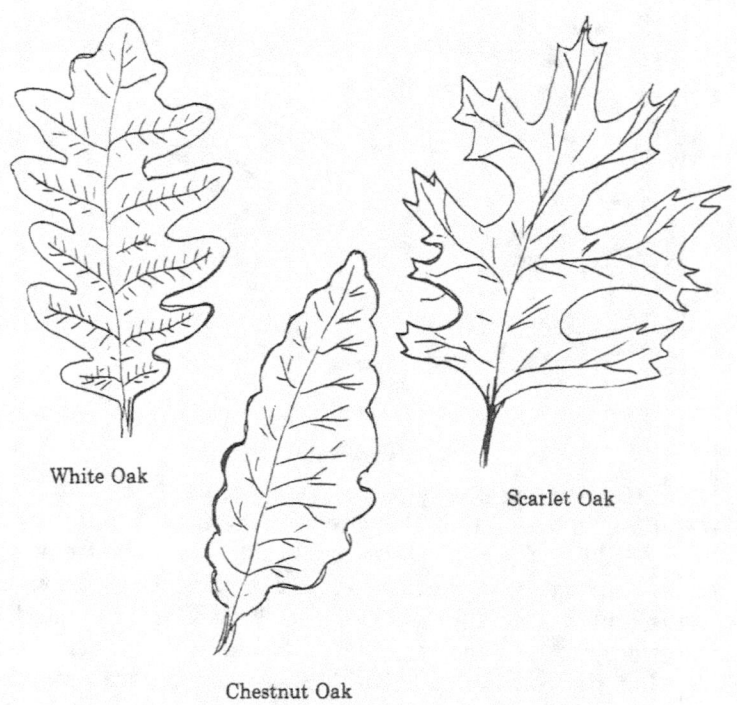

White Oak

Chestnut Oak

Scarlet Oak

Fig. 37

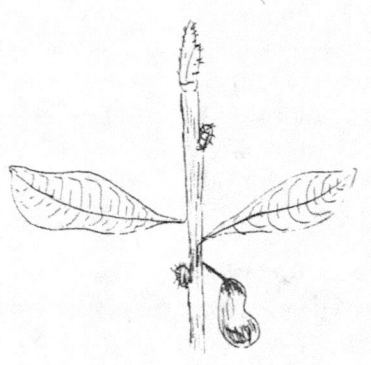

Fig. 38 Pawpaw

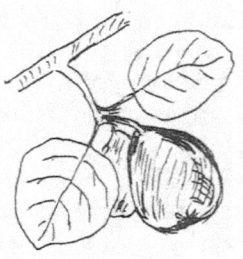

Fig. 39 Wild Pear

46

Fig. 40   Persimmon   Fig. 41   Rose Fruit

PERSIMMON   *Diospyros virginiana*   **Figure 40**
The persimmon is a thin tree with dark deeply furrowed bark.
The flowers are yellow white. The ripe fruit is orange and contains flat seeds. When green the fruit will pucker your mouth
but when ripe it has an interesting sweet flavor. The later in
the season it is picked the more desirable it is.

PINE   *Pinus species*
The inner bark of pine trees can be used as an emergency food,
especially that of the white pine. The seeds of pines are also
edible and can be eaten raw or roasted.

PLUM   *Prunus species*
Wild plums are edible and really more abundant than is suspect-
ed by most people. The chicasaw plum, *Prunus angustifolia* is
red and the Allegheny Sloe plum, *P. alleghaniensis* is deep purple. The wild plum of the east, *P. americana,* is yellow but in
some years produces reddish fruit. These of course can be used
in jams, jellies, and pies or eaten raw.

ROSE   *Rosa species*   **Figure 41**
Roses are easily recognized and are found in open fields and
on the borders of woods. Rose fruits which resemble little apples
are edible and may be used in many ways, raw or cooked. The
pink rose petals may be used to make an interesting tea.

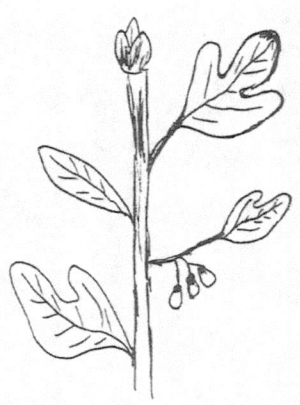

Fig. 42   Sassafras

SASSAFRAS   *Sassafras albidum*   **Figure 42**

The greenish bark, the lobed leaves, and the pleasant smell of the crushed twigs make this tree easily recognized. The leaves may be single, two lobed, or three lobed. They are dark green above and light green below. The tree is found in new woodlands. Its leaves, flowers, stems, twigs, and roots may be used in making tea and flavoring soups. The root is said to be the best for these purposes.

SERVICEBERRY   *Amelanchier species*   **Figure 43**

This juneberry is a shrub that can grow into a large tree if left alone. It develops a white flower which becomes a purple red black berry containing ten seeds. This plant, also known as shadbush, is found in open woods as well as in hedge rows. The berries ripen in late May in the south and ripening progresses northward to Canada when August is the ripening month there. For identification purposes the leaves are somewhat round with sharp toothing, the bark is smooth and grayish. The fruit may be eaten raw or cooked into sauces or made into pies. The berries can also be dried and recovered by simmering in a covered dish.

SPICEBUSH   *Lindera or Benzoic aestivale*   **Figure 44**

This shrub often springs up on long shoots but bush and tree like growth are also common. The flowers appear in the spring

Fig. 43 Serviceberry

Fig. 44 Spicebush

as yellow clusters which change to red berries in the fall. Its leaves are long and similar to choke cherry. It is found in most woodlands and is easy to pass by. Its edible red fruit consists of thin pulp over a large seed. The fruit which has the texture of allspice can be used as a spice in cooking or just chewed as one meanders through the woods. The new bark may also be chewed in the manner one would chew sassafras. A tea may be made by brewing berries, leaves, and twigs.

SPRUCE   *Picea species*

The young shoots of the spruce tree may be used to make beer and the young needles may be eaten raw if one is hard pressed. The spruces are characterized by their sharp pointed needles. The Norway spruce, *Picea abies*, has the longest needles and its twigs are yellow brown. The red spruce, *P. rubens*, has shorter needles and orange brown twig bark with fine hairs. The black spruce, *P. mariana*, is a smaller tree than the other two but quite common.

SUMAC   *Rhus species*   Figure 45

This shrub has coarse soft branches and feather like leaves with numerous pointed leaflets. It bears a terminal cluster of red berry like fruits. The flowering blossoms are small and yellow green. The red yellow fruit of the sumac or sumach is edible and is used to make an excellent tea. For lemonade, pour boiling water over the crushed berries, steep to suitable color, add sugar, cool. The poison sumac resembles the others but has white berries and since only the berries are used there should be no mistakes made here.

TULIP TREE   *Liriodendron tulipfera*

The tulip tree or tulip poplar is the tallest tree in the east. Its leaves are four lobed and light green, turning yellow in the fall. It produces greenish yellow tulip like flowers in the spring. The root of this tree may be used to produce a lemon flavored drink when boiled in water.

WHITE CEDAR   *Thuja occidentalis*

The white cedar or American arbor vitae has the odor of cedar oil when cut. Its twigs and new growth may be used to make tea. Hill people have told me that this tea is good for rheumatism but I don't believe it.

WHITE POPLAR   *Populus alba*

The inner bark of the white poplar can be dried and ground

into flour for making bread. The inner bark can also be cut into strips and eaten raw or cooked. It makes a nice soup.

WITCH HAZEL   *Hamamelis virginiana*

The witch hazel can be found in most woodlands if a diligent search is conducted. Its leaves resemble a small chestnut oak and its fruit is a seed shot from a double husk. The leaves may be boiled to form a strong tea and the seeds may be eaten but they are oily.

YEW   *Taxus canadensis*   Figure 46

The American Yew is a well known ornamental shrub but it can be found in the woods and on the borders of fields. The waxy red berry is sweet and desirable, however the yew does not produce many of these. The seed is reputed to be harmful but there seems to be no evidence for this. The American Yew is a small evergreen shrub resembling the hemlock tree but the yew has larger needles or leaves. The fruit is a fleshy cup and is best eaten right from the bush. Do not eat the bark or needles, spit out the seed.

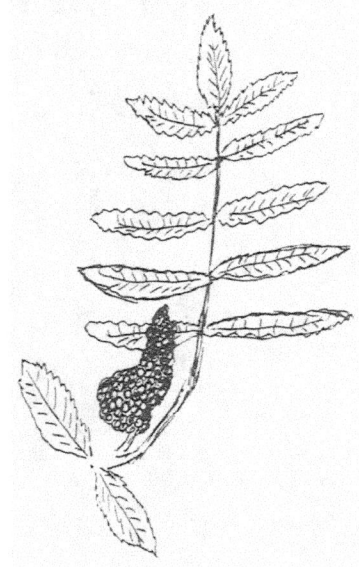

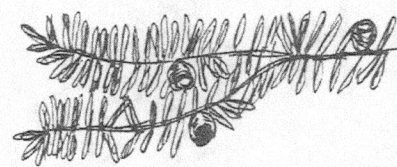

Fig. 45 Sumac   Fig. 46 Yew

V
EDIBLE LOW PLANTS

Mayapple see page 73

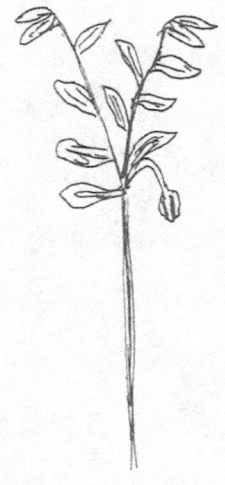

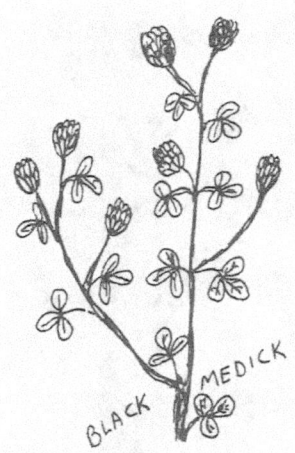

Fig. 47   Bellwort   Fig. 48   Black Medic

BELLWORT   *Uvularia sessilifolia*   Figure 47

The bellwort has solitary or paired pale yellow flowers. Its leaves are grayish beneath and rough on the margins. The plant is found in the open woods. The young shoots may be used as cooked greens.

BEAN   *Phaseolus acutifolius*

The wild bean is unknown to most people. It grows on a vine which climbs over bushes or trails along the ground. It resembles the string bean with its three large oval leaves. Its flowers are purple and these eventually turn into short pods about two inches long.

BLACK MEDIC   *Medicago lupulina*   Figure 48

Although this plant resembles clover it is a member of the pea family. Its clover like blossoms are yellow and they produce a small black coiled seed structure. It is found around meadows and along roadsides. The seeds are edible and have a nice flavor when made into paste and spread on crackers.

BLACK MUSTARD   *Brassica nigra*   Figure 49

The black mustard grows to a height of about five feet. It usually

Fig. 49 Black Mustard   Fig. 50 Burdock

has a hairy stem. The lower leaves are deeply notched, the upper leaves are oblong. Flowers are bright yellow eventually producing a brown pointed seed which has a biting taste. The seeds may be ground and made into a paste for flavoring. The leaves are edible and may be cooked as greens. This plant is also listed as Sinapsis nigra.

BURDOCK   *Arctium minus*   Figure 50

This plant is easily recognized by its large rhubarb like leaves. It has a thick pulpy pithy stem. Its fruit which is burred sticks fast to clothing as well as dogs and cats. The leaves may be peeled and eaten raw or cooked. The flower stalk is also edible. The roots are edible but hard and fibrous and are made more palatable by peeling before preparation. When in bloom the flowers are small reddish violet discs surrounded by hooked bracts. The name clotbur is sometimes given to this plant.

BUTTERCUP   *Ranunculus bulbosus*   Figure 51

Bright yellow flowers bloom on this two foot high plant. Its leaves are longer than broad and are deeply lobed. The roots

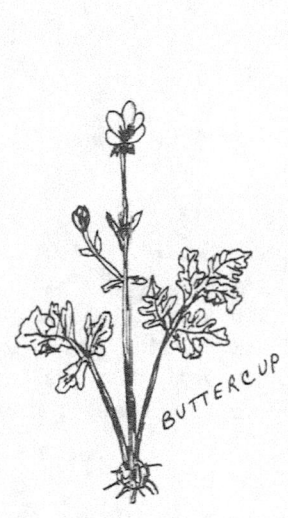

Fig. 51 Buttercup   Fig. 52 Calamus Sweet Flag

are edible when boiled. WARNING: Do not eat the leaves or flowers since they are poisonous.

CALAMUS   *Acorus calamus*   **Figure 52**
The calamus is also known as sweet flag, it resembles the Iris. Its leaves are greenish yellow, its flowers small. The flowers form a spike growing out of the side of a leaf like stalk. The leaves get to be three feet long in large specimens and grow from a closely packed base. The edible root has a ginger or pepper quality to it and may be candied. To candy the root, cut it into thin slices and boil in a thick syrup. Some commercial candies are made from this plant.

CATNIP   *Nepeta cataria*
This member of the mint family is gray and hairy. Its flowers are pale lilac and about a half inch long, forming dense clusters. The leaves are toothed and heart shaped. The leaves of this plant will give a high relish to dishes and sauces.

CHEESES   *Malva rotundifolia*   Figure 53

This plant, also known as mallow, grows in waste lands as well as cultivated gardens. The flat leaves are edible and can be cooked as greens or used in soups. The scalloped fruits can be eaten raw.

CHICKWEED   *Stellaria media*   Figure 54

Chickweed may be found in any season of the year around lawns and in cultivated gardens as well as along roadsides. It is found in bunches and clusters of the stems illustrated. Its stems are weak and reclining with leaves opposite each other. The flowers are small and are borne in terminal leafy clusters. The seeds are edible and the plant may be used as a cooked green.

CHICORY   *Cichorium intybus*   Figure 55

The leaves of the chicory are clustered at the top of a strong taproot. These resemble the dandelion but are thicker and tougher. The plant is best identified by its blue flowers which are sometimes referred to as corn flowers. The plant is found in fields and especially along roadsides and in waste places. Its leaves may be used as a salad green, its roots may be boiled

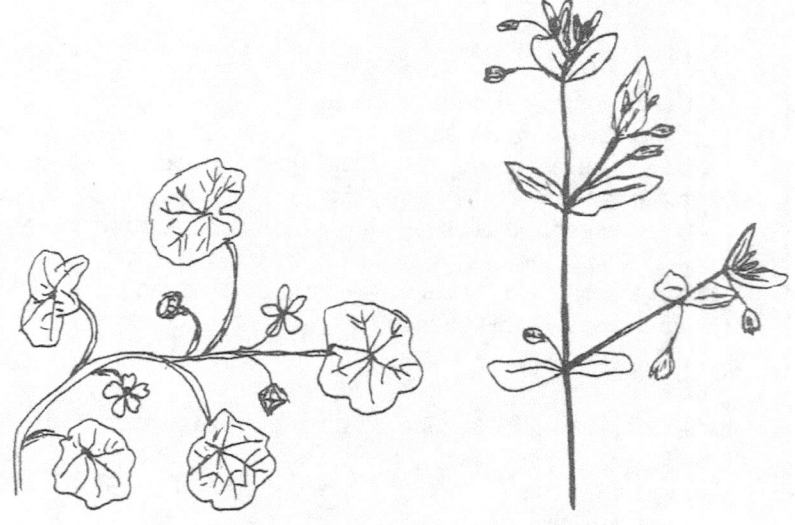

Fig. 53   Cheeses   Fig. 54   Chickweed

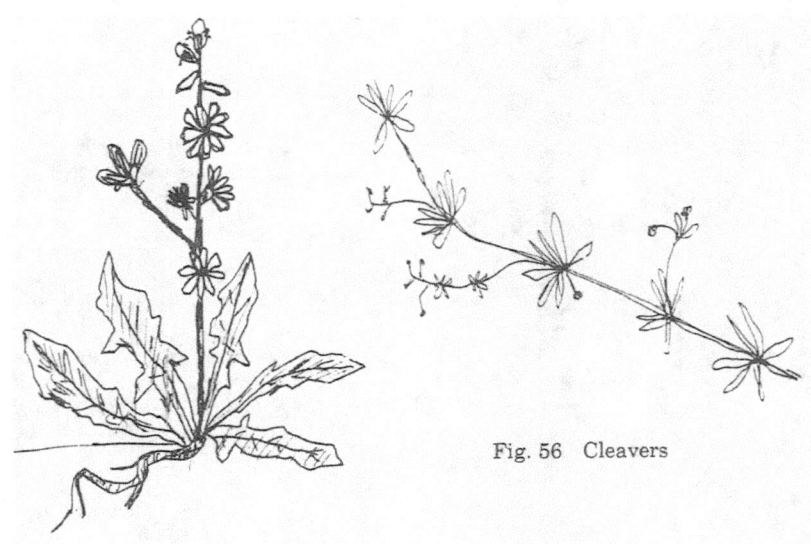

Fig. 56 Cleavers

Fig. 55 Chicory

and eaten. The root may be dried and pulverized and used as a coffee substitute. Young tender leaves may be forced from old roots by watering.

CLEAVERS   *Galium aparine*   Figure 56

Cleavers are named because of the little green balls which cling to cloth and fur. It is also called goose grass and bedstraw. The stems are long and vinelike, the leaves thin. Cleavers grow in woods covering the ground as a green mat. Use it as a cooked green, dry the seeds and make a coffee, dry the plant and make a tea.

COCKLEBUR   *Xanthium strumarium*   Figure 57

This burweed has its sharp pointed fruits close to the central stem. It is a native of waste places and roadsides. Its leaves and shoots may be used as cooked greens. There is some disagreement as to the edibility of the attractive seeds. To be safe, do not eat the seeds.

COLTSFOOT   *Tussilago farfara*   Figure 58

The coltsfoot is recognized by its yellow club like flowers which

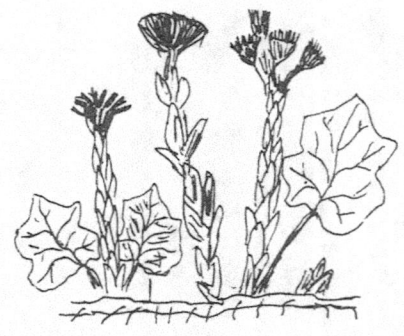

Fig. 57 Cocklebur   Fig. 58 Coltsfoot

bloom before the leaves appear. It has a fleshy stem. The coltsfoot is found along new roadcuts and in other areas of damp clay. Its leaves may be dried and then slowly burned, the ashes being used for a tasty seasoning. Extracts of this plant are used in making a cough medicine called coltsfoot candy.

CLOVER

RED CLOVER   *Trifolium pratense*
SWEET CLOVER   *Melilotus officinalis*
WHITE CLOVER   *Trifolium repens*
YELLOW CLOVER *Trifolium agrarium*

The seeds and flower heads of the clovers are edible. Use these in salads. I have eaten the leaves of clovers and found them difficult to digest.

**CREEPING
SNOWBERRY**   *Chiogenes hispidula*   **Figure 59**

This trailing vine has the flavor of wintergreen, its berries are white and covered with small hairs. The berry is found on the lower sides of the vine like branches. The berries are edible raw or cooked.

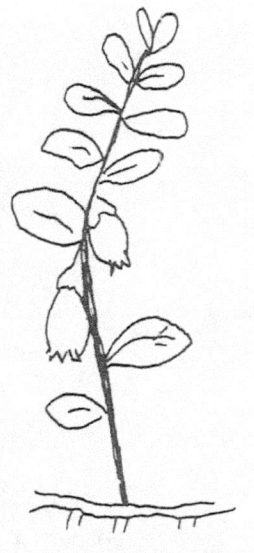

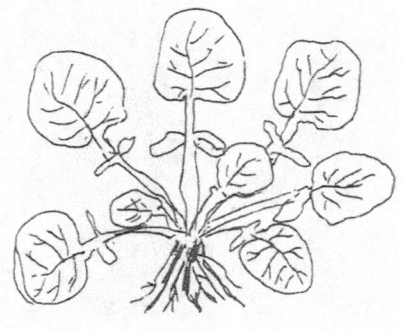

Fig. 60 Winter Cress
Yellow Rocket

Fig. 59 Snowberry

CRESS

PENNY CRESS   *Thlaspi arvense*
WATER CRESS   *Cardamine rotundifolia*
WINTER CRESS   *Barbarea vulgaris*   **Figure 60**
The various cress plants grow in large clumps of bright green leaves which remain fresh for a long time, the winter cress being available all winter. The leaf terminus is rounded. The stem is stout and shoots up early in the spring and bears elongating clusters of yellow flowers in the winter cress. Cress is found in low ground near streams and in inhabited areas. The plant is especially good in spring. Use it as a salad green, as cooked greens, or as an ingredient in soup.

DANDELION   *Taraxacum officinale*   **Figure 61**
The Yellow flowers of the dandelion are familiar to everyone, especially to lawn fanciers as they try to get at the flowers before they go to seed. Some dandelions are brown seeded and some are red seeded. They all have long fleshy taproots which may be dried and pulverized to make a palatable coffee. The

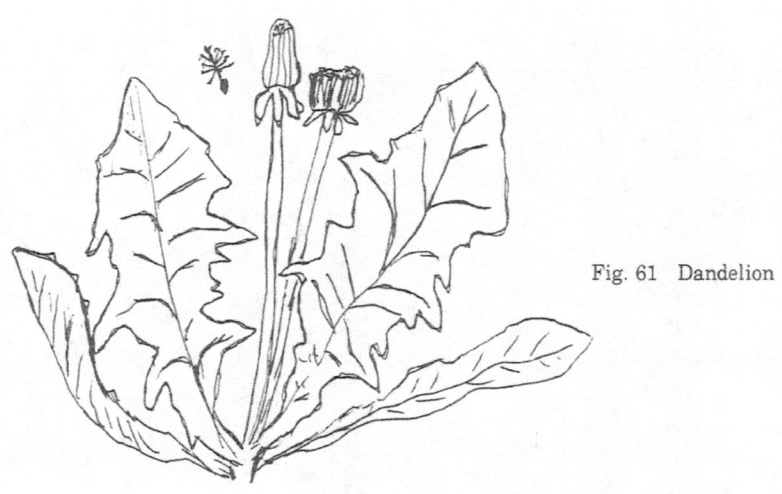

Fig. 61 Dandelion

young leaves may be used as either salad greens or cooked greens. The green leaves may be used for making a tea. The blossoms are used for making wine.

DAISY   *Chrysanthemum leucanthemum*   **Figure 62**
The white daisy or ox eye daisy is familiar to everyone. It is a composite flower with aggressive roots and is found in dry fields. It is smelly and to eat its edible leaves one must acquire a taste for its odor. The leaves may be used as cooked greens; the odor becomes less noticeable after a few eatings.

Fig. 62 Daisy

DAYFLOWER *Commelina communis* **Figure 63**

The dayflower has a small blue flower consisting of one pale petal and two dark petals. It grows rapidly in a sprawling manner. The leaves are parallel veined. The plant is found in shaded areas or woodlands and hedge rows. It is a frequent visitor to domestic gardens. The plant may be cooked and served as greens. Other names for it are the common dayflower and spreading dayflower.

DOCK

CURLED DOCK *Rumex crispus* **Figure 64**

This is a perennial plant with a large thick taproot. It has lance shaped leaves which are wavy or curled at the margins. It bears small greenish flowers which are borne in ascending fashion. The fruit at the top of the plant is reddish brown when ripe and resembles coffee grounds. The new leaves of this and all docks are wholesome and may be used as cooked greens. The plant loses much of its bulk when cooked and so ample collecting must be made to assure a mess.

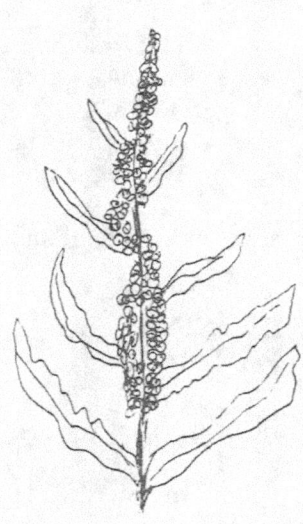

Fig. 63 Dayflower   Fig. 64 Curled Dock

Fig. 65 Sour Dock   Fig. 66 Evening Primrose

SOUR DOCK   *Rumex acetosella*   **Figure 65**

This sour dock is easily recognized by its arrowhead like leaves containing a sour juice, hence also the name sorrel and chow chow. The branching stalks of tiny flowers are followed by tiny seeds. The seed stalks develop the second year. The male flowers are yellowish and the female flowers are reddish brown. This plant is a sign of acid soil and is found in fields and lawns and on the edges of properties. Use the leaves in green salads, cook them as greens, or simmer the leaves in water to make a hot or cold lemonade.

EVENING
PRIMROSE   *Oenothera biennis*   **Figure 66**

The mature primrose stands from two to four feet high with flowers about an inch in diameter which open in late afternoon. The flowers which appear in the second year are blunt and light yellow in color. The leaves are elliptical with sparsely toothed margins. It is found in thickets and other dry habitats. The leaves of the young plant are palatable peeled and eaten raw. The root may be used as a vegetable and is excellent in stews.

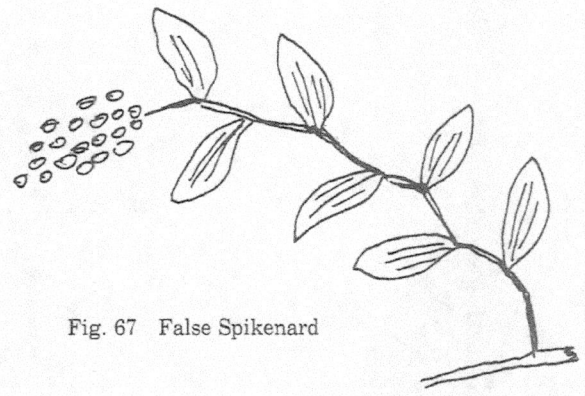

Fig. 67   False Spikenard

FALSE SPIKENARD   *Smilacina racemosa*   Figure 67

This false Solomon's Seal or Solomon's Plume produces an edible reddish berry in the fall. It does not have the underground stem system of the real Solomon's Seal, hence its name. Its numerous leaves are hairy edged and veiny. It reaches a height of about two feet. It is sometimes listed as plume lily in reference works.

FERN

BRACKEN FERN   *Pteris aquilina*   Figure 68

This is a coarse fern with solitary or scattered young stalks. Its base is covered with rusty felt and has an extensive creeping rootstalk. It is found in open woods and pastures. The young fronds are edible when unrolled. Young shoots may be cooked and eaten, the roots or rhizomes may also be boiled and eaten or dried and made into meal and then into bread. The plant can also be used to make a good beer.

OSTRICH FERN   *Matteuccia struthiopteris*   Figure 69

The young fronds of this fern form dense vaselike clumps which rise from a free forking rootstock. Last years fronds resemble thick dark brown feathers, the new fronds bear brown scales with a feather like leafy summit. The leaves of this plant look like ostrich feathers, hence the name. The new leaves rise from circular clumps which look like fiddleheads. These fiddleheads are edible raw or cooked. Boil them in salt water and serve

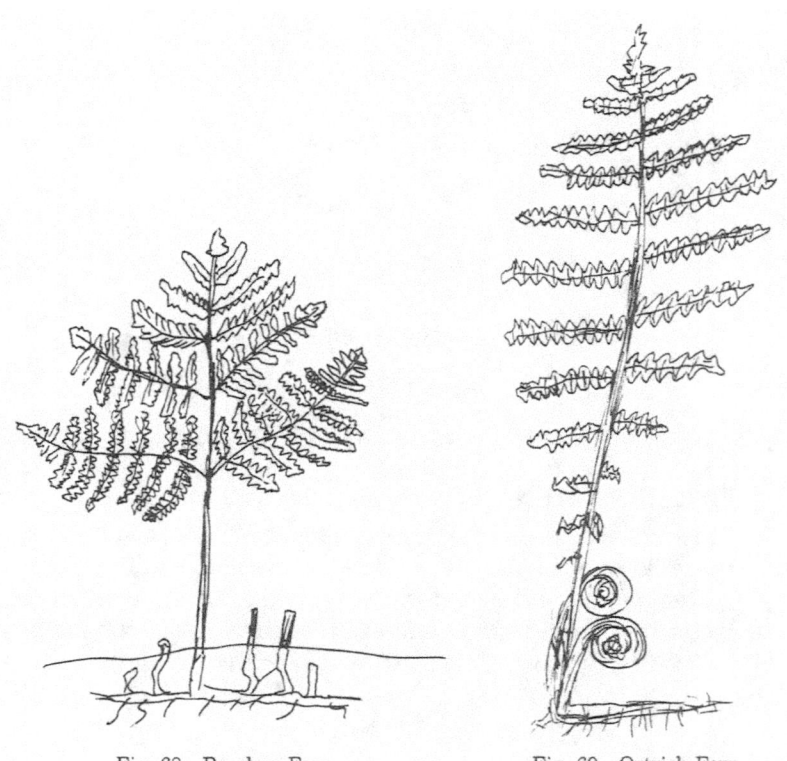

Fig. 68   Bracken Fern   Fig. 69   Ostrich Fern

with bacon drippings. Check out stream beds and rich woods
for this fern in the fall and mark the spot well, return in spring
and begin your harvest.

FIREWEED   *Epilobium angustifolium*   **Figure 70**

The fireweed grows to a height of three to five feet. Its flowers
are about an inch in diameter and are bright purple in color.
The fireweed seeds bear long white hairs. The plant is found
in open woods and thickets and is abundant in burnt over areas
from which it gets its name. Use the leaves for tea or boil the
leaves and stems for cooked greens. The plant may be dried
and used as an herb.

GINGER   *Asarum canadense*   **Figure 71**

The wild ginger plant appears as a two leaved plant with the

Fig. 70   Fireweed

Fig. 71   Ginger

leaves flattening out at the top of the stem. The leaves are heart shaped and about five inches wide. This woodland plant bears a solitary three pointed brownish purple flower. The root has a strong ginger flavor and can be munched on raw or boiled with brown sugar and preserved as a candy. The root can be added to stews or used in other forms of cooking. A tea can be made from the root by boiling only a few minutes.

GOLDENROD — *Solidago odora* — Figure 72
The sweet goldenrod is a slender plant reaching three feet in height. Its flowers are yellowish and tend to be on one side of the plant. Its leaves are narrow and dotted with small glands which yield a pleasant odor. Either the dried seed heads or the dried leaves will make an acceptable tea, or both together.

GROUND CHERRY — *Physalis species* — Figure 73
The ground cherry grows to about a foot in height but its drooping nature gives one the impression that it is much bigger. Its fruit is easily recognized being a cherry or small tomato encased in a lantern like paper husk, hence it is known as Chinese or Japanese lantern as well as husk tomato. The leaves and the stems of the plant are covered with short hairs and the

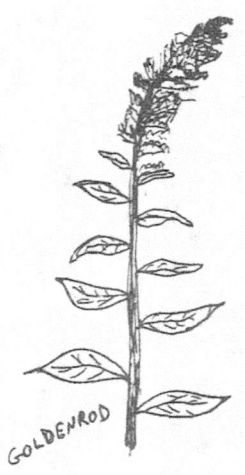

Fig. 72 Goldenrod   Fig. 73 Ground Cherry

joints are slightly swollen. The plant is found on open soil. The cherry may be eaten raw or cooked or put in preserves. It is worth seeking and tasting.

GROUND IVY   *Nepeta hederacea*   Figure 74

This creeping member of the mint family forms mats along hedge rows. It is also known as Gill Over The Ground. Its flowers are small and lavender. The leaves of ground ivy are round with blunt tooth edges; these may be dried and used to make tea.

HEDGE MUSTARD   *Sisymbrium officinale*

This is a common weed of hayfields. It develops a thin row of seeds in a pod. The leaves are deeply toothed and its yellow flowers are small. Use as a salad or cooked green. Use it to spice up sauces.

HONEWORT   *Cryptotaenia canadensis*   Figure 75

The five petaled flowers of the honewort are small and inconspicuous. Its fruit is composed of dry seeds and its leaves are long stalked with coarse toothing. The dry seeds are about an inch long and split into halves easily. It is a native of moist woodlands. The leaves may be used as greens and in soups.

Fig. 74 Ground Ivy   Fig. 75 Honewort

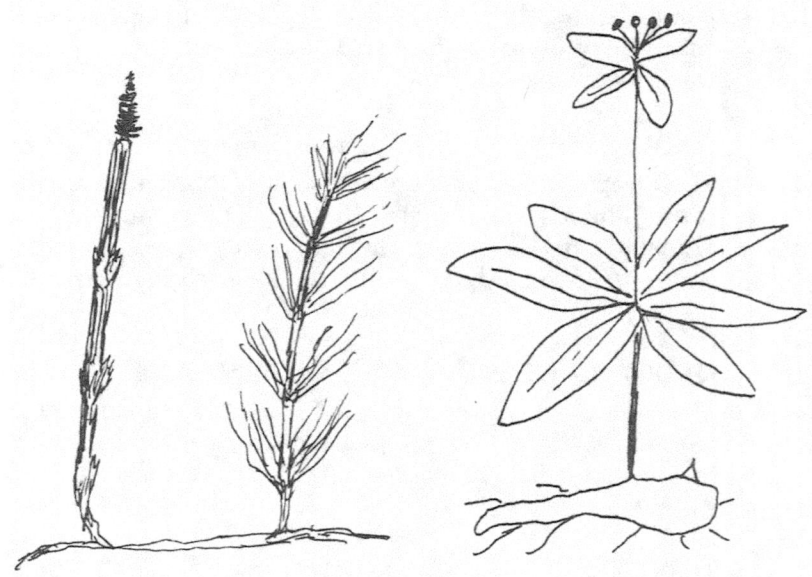

Fig. 76 Horsetail   Fig. 77 Indian Cucumber

The root is edible and should be cooked. Stems and leaves may be used in salads or dried as an herb.

HORSETAIL *Equisetum fluviatile* **Figure 76**
This pipe joint grass is easily recognized. It and its relative the scouring rush, *Equisetum hyemale,* may be cooked as greens when young. The shoots may also be peeled and eaten raw. Do not use the older plants or plants which have been cut for more than a day for food.

INDIAN CUCUMBER *Medeola virginiana* **Figure 77**
The Indian Cucumber is a single stemmed woodland plant which stands erect. It has a rosette of leaves halfway up the stem and another smaller set near the top. In autumn the green leaves become purplish. The pale yellow flowers near the apex of the stalk become purple black berries in the fall. The long white brittle crispy roots are edible raw or cooked. It is delicious raw and it is easy to extract with little digging. It may be gathered at any time but may be difficult to find in the winter when the leaves disappear. Once the root shape is identified and the

crisp cucumber like taste tried, it will be a part of the memory forever.

JEWEL WEED *Impatiens biflora*

The spotted touch me not or snapweed has orange flowers with purple spots. If you touch it when mature it will shoot out its seeds. When young, the stems are edible as cooked greens or raw for its high moisture content.

KNOTWEED *Polygonum cuspidatum* **Figure 78**

The Japanese Knotweed is an erect shrub reaching to eight feet in height. It is recognized by its similarity to bamboo. Its leaves are stalked and eggshaped with a squared base. Its flowers are greenish white. It is found in waste places along roadsides, and on once inhabited land. The young leaves may be used as a salad green or cooked green. The roots may be cooked and eaten at any season of the year. Even though it is of shrub quality since it grows new shoots each year it is placed in this section of low plants.

LAMB'S QUARTERS *Chenopodium album* **Figure 79**

The leaves of lamb's quarters are alternate and long stemmed with angular toothing especially near the base. When picking

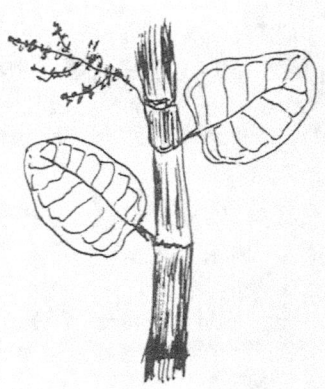

Fig. 78   Knotweed

Fig. 79   Lamb's Quarters   Fig. 80   Marsh Marigold

the leaves one will notice the mealy character of the undersides. Older plants bear scalloped green flowers in clusters which turn to small black seeds. The lower leaves of the plant often have purple blotches caused by a fungus. The plant is found as a weed in almost all gardens, around buildings, and in roadside situations. It is a delicious plant when boiled as greens. The seeds are edible and may be pounded into meal. Avoid the leaves tainted with the red or violet fungus. The orach, Atriplex sp., resembles lamb's quarters and is easily mistaken for it. It is a common plant of the seacoasts and delicious as a cooked green. It has a slightly salt taste and is therefore referred to as saltbush.

MARSH MARIGOLD   *Caltha palustris*   **Figure 80**
The leaves of this cowslip are kidney shaped, scalloped around the edges and edible. They and the young stems may be used as cooked greens. The flowers of the plant are orange yellow and are found in leafy clusters on hollow stems. The plant is native to wet meadows and swamps, hence its other name of meadow bright. Besides the edible leaves and stems the flower buds may be pickled. Absolutely do not eat the plant raw.

Fig. 81   Mayapple   Fig. 82   Milkweed

MAYAPPLE   *Podophyllum peltatum*   **Figure 81**

This plant, also known as mandrake, is recognized by its umbrella like stance in woodlands. Its flower is white and large, being carried between the forks of the two large leaves. The apple is a yellow berry. The leaves are deeply divided into coarse toothed lobes. Use the apple raw or in jellies. The fruit is ripe when it is yellow. Do not eat the leaves or the roots since they are poisonous.

MILKWEED   *Asclepias syriaca*   **Figure 82**

The milkweed or silkweed is common and easily recognized by its milky juice. Its leaves are broad and oblong, its flowers are showy and near the middle of summer turn into little pods which when mature produce a silken seed. The milkweed is found in open places, along fence rows, and along roadsides. The new tender shoots may be used as cooked greens, the young pods may be eaten raw or cooked. The pods which have a nutty flavor are excellent with meat. The flower buds may be cooked, these are claimed by many to be the most tasty part of the plant.

MINT   *Mentha candensis*
PEPPERMINT   *Mentha piperita*

SPEARMINT   *Mentha spicata*

Mints have square stems and opposite leaves which contain a fragrant oil. The plant oil can be used for flavoring. Leaves may be roasted or eaten directly. A bit of salt sets the flavor off nicely. Boil the leaves for mint tea or dry them for herb use. Pennyroyal, Hedeoma sp., is a mint used in making tea. It is found in dry fields and is well known in many localities.

MUGWORT   *Artemisia vulgaris*

The mugwort or wormwood leaves may be used for flavoring drinks or they may be dried for use as an aromatic culinary herb.

BLACK
NIGHTSHADE   *Solanum nigrum*   Figure 83

This is a low branched and spreading annual which bears small white flowers in clusters. It may be described as bushy branched. It is found in dry open soil, at the borders of woods, along roadsides, and on cultivated land. The berries are black and may be made into pies or eaten raw. The young shoots and leaves are also edible. Do not confuse this plant with the climbing nightshade, also known as the deadly nightshade, whose berries are toxic but not necessarily as fatal as the name implies. The berries of the deadly nightshade are red and should be avoided. Don't eat either plant unless you are sure of its identity.

NETTLE   *Urtica species*   Figure 84

The nettles are erect plants with coarsely toothed strongly ribbed leaves. The lower leaves are covered with fine stinging bristles. The flowers which are borne in small greenish clusters are found in the upper axils of the plant in summer. The leaves may be collected with gloves to prevent getting stung. They are excellent as cooked greens, cook for about five minutes, do not overcook them. The leaves loose their stinging quality upon cooking. Especially good is the stinging nettle, *Urtica dioica*.

WILD ONION   *Allium cernuum*   Figure 85

There are many names for the wild onion and many varieties of the basic form. All forms have a bulb at the base with tubular

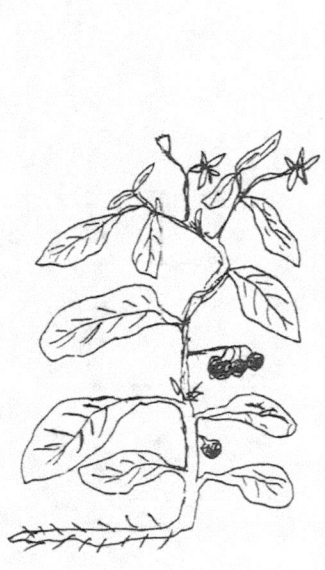

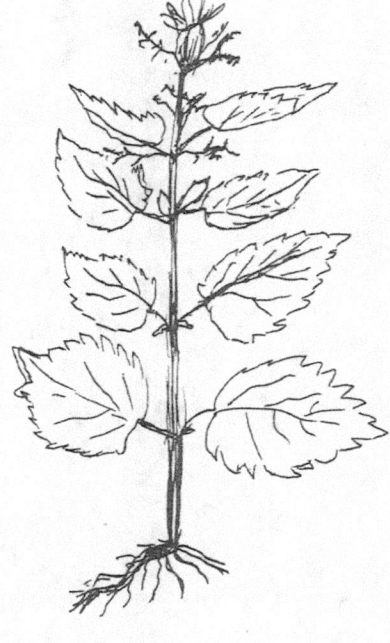

Fig. 83   Black Nightshade   Fig. 84   Stinging Nettle

leaves. The flowers are pinkish white. Plants of this nature have been also called wild garlic, wild leek, meadow garlic, and field garlic. Use these in soups and stews. If you eat it raw it will taste good and strong for the moment as well as days later. The plant can be dried and stored for future use.

ORPINE   *Sedum telephium*   **Figure 86**

This weed grows to about two feet in height and bears succulent leaves crowded spirally around a stem. Its flowers are small and are from reddish to white. It has fleshy tuber like roots and is native of damp fields, roadsides, and other weed habitats. It can be used as a salad green while young. The leaves and stems can also be used as a cooked green. The roots or tubers may be boiled and served with salt and a dash of vinegar or pickled for future use.

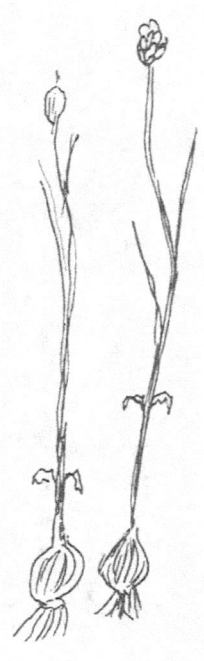

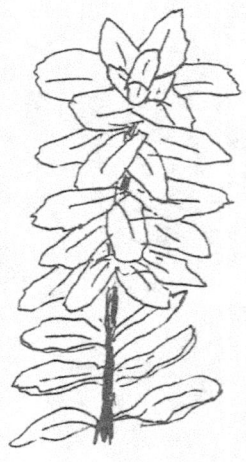

Fig. 85   Wild Onion   Fig. 86   Orpine

OXALIS   *Oxalis acetosella*   **Figure 87**

This sour grass is found around your yard as well as in the woods. It has clover like leaves which are notched. The flowers have five petals and are yellow in the species above. Other edible species have white or pink petals. The whole plant is acid to the taste, hence its other name of wood sorrel. Use it raw in salads. The onion like tubers may be eaten raw or boiled.

PARSNIP (WILD)   *Pastinaca sativa*   **Figure 88**

This is the wild form of the cultivated parsnip. It is identified by its tall hollow branching stem which is deeply grooved all the way to its tip. The leaves are pinnately compound and coarsely toothed with lobed segments. The flowers are small and yellow and are in large compound flat topped groups. The seeds are flattened. The plant and seeds have a distinct unpleasant odor. Wild parsnips are found along roadways, railroad beds, and formerly cultivated areas. The root is a taproot, long and narrow

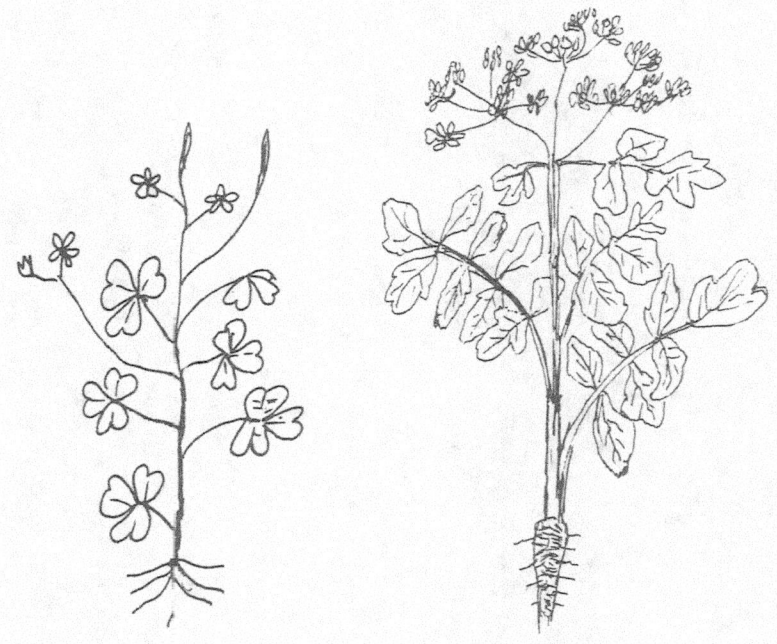

Fig. 87 Oxalis   Fig. 88 Wild Parsnip

and it is edible raw or cooked. See notes on water hemlock and poison hemlock also.

PEPPERGRASS *Lepidium virginicum*

Peppergrass leaves form rosettes in spring and are cress like. They bear minute white flowers in spike like clusters. Seed pods are flat, circular, and similar to shepherd's purse seeds in growth pattern. Use as a salad green or as a garnish. The seeds are tasty.

PIGWEED *Amaranthus retroflexus* Figure 89

The seeds and flowers of the *amaranth* have a strawlike character. Its leaves and stems are often hairy. This plant is found in the garden as a weed and can usually be identified by its red roots, hence also the name of redroot. I prefer the name *amaranth* or green *amaranth* by which it is also known since pigweed is not savory and the plant is one of the most delicious

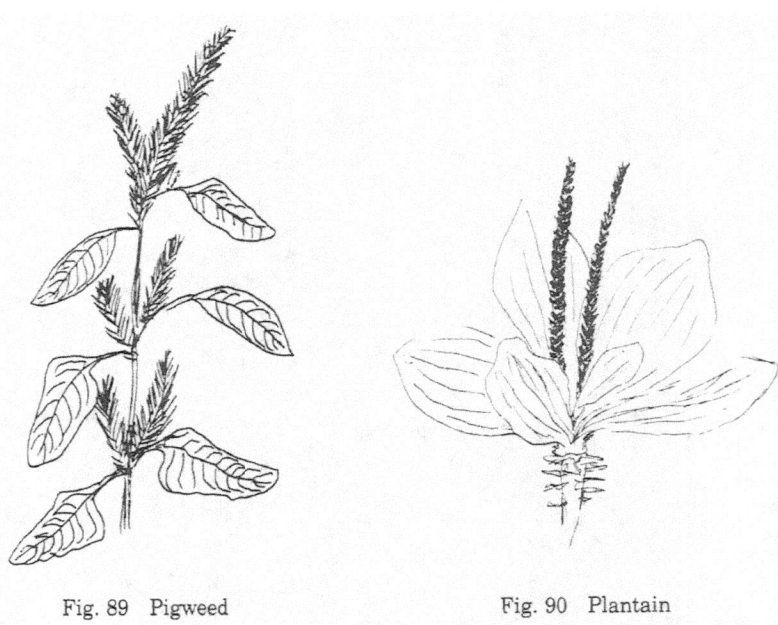

Fig. 89 Pigweed

Fig. 90 Plantain

Fig. 91 Pokeweed

Fig. 92 Purslane

of the wild ones. The seeds are edible and the young shoots and leaves may be eaten as a cooked green.

PLANTAIN   *Plantago major*   Figure 90

This is the common dooryard plantain which has broad leaves and strong stringy fibers in them. In spring the young leaves may be used as cooked greens. Regardless of preparation the plant is tough and if eaten raw causes indigestion in the strongest of stomachs.

POKEWEED   *Phytolacca americana*   Figure 91

The pokeweed is a tall coarse plant with elliptical pointed leaves which reach lengths of ten inches. The tall stems are tinted purple. The plant is also called inkberry by many since its fruit is in the form of dark purple berries which are found in clusters atop the stems. The pokeweed is found in open soil, in wood clearings, along roadsides, and in cultivated gardens. The young shoots may be cooked as greens. This is probably the most famous of the edible wild plants. Some prefer to throw away the first cooking water and do a second quick boiling. The fruit of poke is edible but the seeds are poisonous so do not eat the fruit. The root is poisonous and so is the older stem.

PURSLANE   *Portulaca oleracea*   Figure 92

This succulent is a common visitor to cultivated gardens and fields since its seeds are a common impurity in seed packets. It is a matted creeping herb with moist looking stems and very fleshy narrowly wedge shaped reddish green opposite leaves. The flowers have yellow petals. The top of the seed pod lifts off like a cap. Use the plant as cooked greens, use in soups, or pickle it. The seeds are edible. The stems may be eaten raw for their moisture but let us hope that one is never that thirsty.

QUACKGRASS   *Agropyron repens*   Figure 93

Quackgrass has slender wiry white roots with tenacious joints. It spreads by this creeping rhizome. Its leaves are flat and dark green. The erect stalk terminates in a finger like spike with alternate notches of spikelets. The grass is found on open ground and is considered an obnoxious weed in cultivated ground. A good bread may be prepared by drying and grinding the roots.

Fig. 93   Quackgrass   Fig. 94   Queen Anne's Lace

QUEEN
ANNE'S LACE   *Daucus carota*   **Figure 94**

The bird's nest appearance of the flowers of this plant are easily
recognized.The plant may grow to three feet in height with leaves
cut in fernlike fashion. Flowers are compound white and usually
have a purple or red flower at its center. Queen Anne's Lace
is found in dry pastures and fields which are returning back
to nature. The root is edible and was the source of our present
domestic carrot. This plant resembles the poison water hemlock.
Refer to the notes on the low hemlocks in section II.

RICE   *Zizania species*   **Figure 95A**

The Indian Rice or Wild Rice is a grass of lakes and other water
margins. It is similar to oats with its loose husk having a long
bristle at the top. The grain is dark brown, less than an inch
long, and falls from the husk when ripe so it must be gathered
at the right time which is just as the grains start to fall. Its
greatest abundance is in the western Great Lakes region and
if a northern lake is named Rice Lake it is after this grain
and not somebody named Rice. It may be cooked as you would
ordinary rice.

 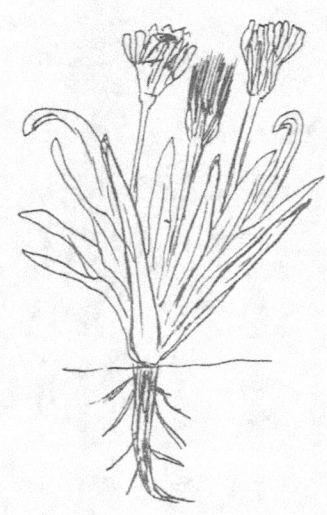

Fig. 95A Wild Rice   Fig. 95B Salsify

SALSIFY   *Tragopogon porrifolius*   **Figure 95B**
A milky juice is secreted from the broad grassblade leaves of
this goat's beard or oyster plant. The flowering stem develops
in the second year with flowers resembling large dandelions
and purple in color. Closely related species which are also edible
have yellow flowers. The plant is native to fields and roadsides.
The roots can be eaten throughout the winter and are usually
boiled or fried. New spring shoots are used as cooked greens.

SHEPHERD'S
PURSE   *Capsella bursapastoris*   **Figure 96**
Leaves of this mustard plant are basal with various lobes as
well as sharp toothing. Its lower leaves have long tapering bases
and its stem leaves are entire with clasping bases. The flowers
are small and white growing out from the tall stems. The fruit
forms a sort of triangle. Shepherd's Purse may be found in lawns
and gardens as well as waste places and areas once occupied
by man. Use as cooked greens.

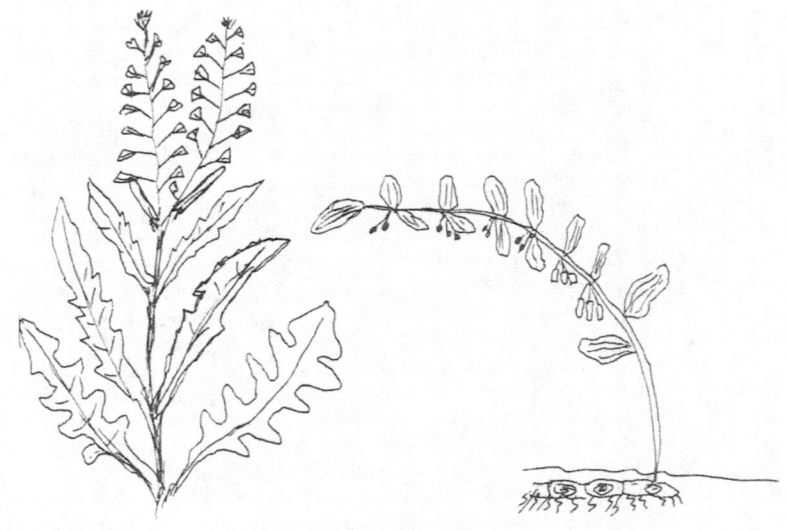

Fig. 96   Shepherd's Purse   Fig. 97   Solomon's Seal

SOLOMON'S SEAL   *Polygonatum species*   **Figure 97**
Flowers of the solomon's seal are greenish white and grow on a stalk from three to five feet high. The plant is often bent over and it has alternate smooth leaves from the axils of which the flowers rise. The fruit is in the form of bluish berries. The plant gets its name from the scars on its underground stem. It is native of the woodland. Use by boiling the young shoots and roots. This plant is rare and should really not be used unless there is some sort of gourmet emergency.

SPEEDWELL   *Veronica species*   **Figure 98**
Speedwell is a sprawling perennial with lavender blue flowers. It is found in many varieties, especially common in bird's eye speedwell. Its leaves are broad and hairy and have coarsely rounded teeth. The leaves are opposite each other on the stems. The plant is found in dry open woods as well as on roadsides and in abandoned fields. It forms large colonies due to its trailing habit. Use the leaves for making tea.

Fig. 98 Speedwell

Fig. 99 Spiderwort

SPIDERWORT   *Tradescantia virginica*   **Figure 99**

This is one of the many edible spiderworts. The flowers are radial, that is, arranged in circular fashion. Their color is violet to white. Leaves are long and narrow and appear bluish green. The plant is found in grasslands and open woods. Cook the young stems and leaves as greens.

SPRING BEAUTY   *Claytonia caroliniana*   **Figure 100**

This member of the portulaca family has stems several inches high which have pairs of long narrow leaves. The flowers are about a half inch in diameter and are white to pink. The root system is in the form of a tuber. The plant is found in open woods and grasslands. The bulbs or tubers are edible.

STRAWBERRY   *Fragaria virginiana*   **Figure 101**

The wild strawberry easily outclasses its domestic relatives in flavor. The leaves which are covered with fine hairs grow directly from the roots. They are three in number and are broad and saw toothed. The flower is white. The berries progress from green to white and then finally to beautiful red. The berry is of course, edible. The leaves may be used to brew a pleasant tea.

Fig. 100   Spring Beauty   Fig. 101   Strawberry

SUNFLOWER
(JERUSALEM ARTICHOKE)   *Helianthus tuberosus*

Once I had discovered the Jerusalem artichoke, *Helianthus tuberosus,* it seemed to be everywhere. These sunflowers are quite common. The tubers or roots are excellent roasted, boiled or pickled. They are found along railroad tracks, roadsides, and in waste places, look for them.

TANSY   *Tanacetum vulgare*   Figure 102

The tansy grows to a height of almost three feet in good soil but is usually found to be about a foot and a half tall. It is perennial and the flower heads are numerous with a flat topped grouping. The flowers are yellow. The leaves of the tansy are large and divided in a fern type pattern. The plant is found mostly in once lived in areas and is most easily recognized by its yellow button heads. The plant is highly aromatic and has been used in folk medicine for centuries. Use it as an herb or to make a bitter tea.

TEABERRY   *Gaultheria procumbens*   Figure 103

This wintergreen is a low plant creeping beneath other foliage near the ground surface. It has erect branches from three to six inches high. The aromatic leaves which are rigid or stiff

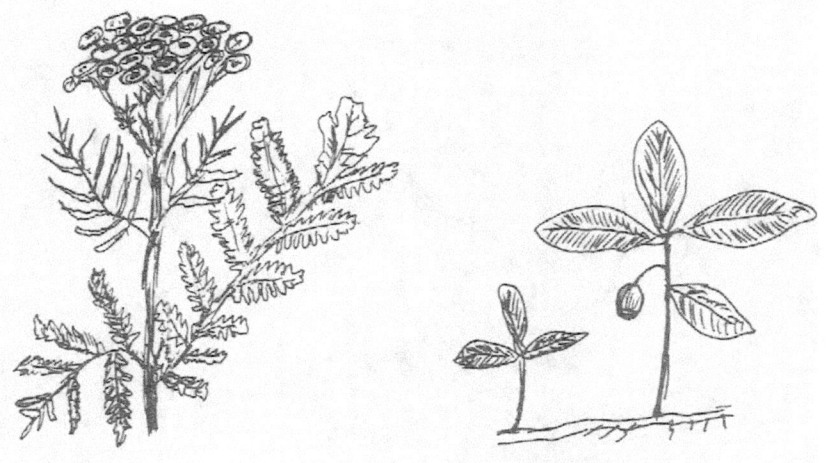

Fig. 102   Tansy   Fig. 103   Teaberry

are colored dark glossy green. The oval leaves have small bristle tipped teeth. The red berry hangs on the stem all winter. The plant is found in hilly and mountainous surroundings frequently in association with evergreens. The berry may be eaten raw or used in cooked dishes. A tea may be prepared from the leaves.

THISTLE

COMMON THISTLE
(JOHNNY GREEN)   *Cirsium vulgare*
Remove thorns from the leaves and eat raw or cooked. The stalk may be peeled and also eaten raw or cooked.

SOW THISTLE   *Sonchus* species   Figure 104
This coarse prickly plant grows to a height of four feet. Its leaves have prickly margins and are often prominently lobed. The flowers are bright yellow. The plant secretes a milky bitter juice. It is found as a weed in cultivated land and along roadsides. Use only young and tender plants as a salad green or cooked green.

STAR THISTLE   *Centaurea* species   Figure 105
The young stems and leaves may be eaten raw or cooked on both the sow and star thistles.

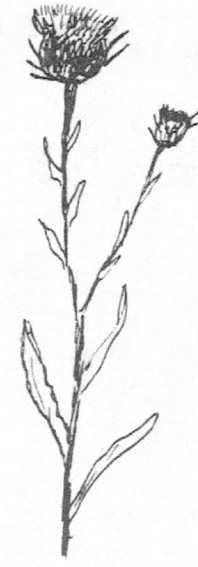

Fig. 104   Sow Thistle   Fig. 105   Star Thistle

TOOTHWORTS   *Dentaria species*

The cut leaved toothwort, *Dentaria laciniata* and the two leaved toothwort, *Dentaria diphylla*, are members of the mustard family. The roots are mustardy and hence the name pepperroots. The edible roots are toothed or highly crinkled and may be used as a relish.

TRILLIUM   *Trillium grandiflorum*

The leaves of this well known plant can be used as greens. Please, only in an emergency.

VETCH   *Vicia species*   Figure 106

The vetch is a member of the pea family and has the same tendril climbing habit originating at the tip of its pinnate leaves. The vetch flowers are slightly less than an inch long and are found in sparse groups. They are purple. It is a plant of moist woodlands and tall brush. The seeds are edible and can be used in soups or in breads much the same as caraway seeds.

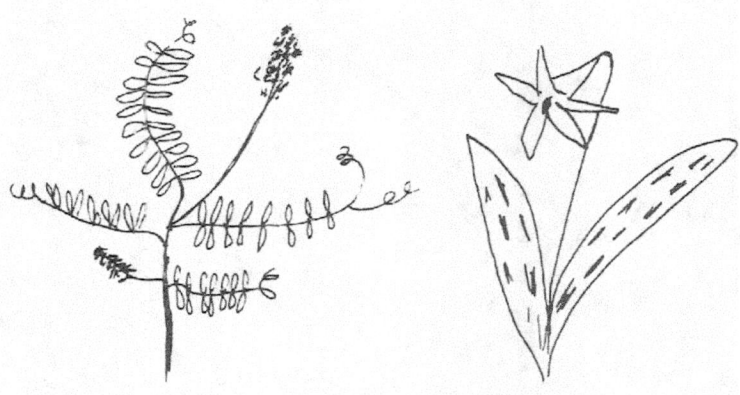

Fig. 106   Vetch   Fig. 107   Trout Lily

YELLOW ADDER'S
TONGUE   *Erythronium americanum*   **Figure 107**

The fawn lily or trout lily rises as a single flower stalk bearing a yellow bell shaped flower. Its leaves are two or three, elliptical and deeply mottled. It is a native of woodlands. Use the bulbous root as a cooked vegetable. Use the leaves as cooked greens.

VI
NOTES ON FUNGI AND LICHENS

Bear's Head fungus *Hydnum capuursi*

PUFFBALLS *Lycoperdon and Calvatia species*

All puffballs are edible and should only be collected when young and firm. Any dark colored puffball should not be eaten. Young puffballs can be cooked directly. The giant puffball, *Calvatia gigantea*, should be peeled before frying or cooking. Puffballs are delicious sliced and fried or cut into bits and mixed with scrambled eggs. Be sure you have a puffball and not a mushroom in the button stage.

MUSHROOMS

Although there are more edible mushrooms than poisonous mushrooms it is best to keep away from them entirely unless you are personally acquainted with someone who will show them to you and eat them with you. Eating them on the basis of handbook descriptions are at best hazardous. Do not believe folk ways for finding out if the mushrooms are edible or not. One of these popular superstitions concerning mushrooms is that i they are boiled with a silver coin and the coin turns black the mushrooms are poisonous. Don't try any such foolishness, buy your mushrooms commercially.

There are two great edible species that once recognized are easy to recognize again. These are the meadow mushroom *Agaricu arvensis* and *Agaricus campestris* which is found in pasture: and cow meadows in and around cow manure, and the earl!

Fig. 108   Early Inky Mushroom   Fig. 109   Edible Morel

inky mushroom found around dead or decayed stumps and are called by the collectors as "stumpies." Again I must emphasize, don't eat them without the approval and guidance of someone who does not rely upon superstition for his source of information. These species of mushrooms are edible and found in Pennsylvania and New York. Do not attempt to eat them unless you are sure of yourself.

Agaricus arvensis	field mushroom
Agaricus campestris	meadow mushroom
Armillaria mellea	honey mushroom
Cantharellus cibarius	chanterelle
Clavaria pulchra	yellow club
Clavaria umbonatus	grayling
Collybia radicata	root mushroom
Collybia velutipes	velvet collybia
Coprinus atramentarius	ink cap
Coprinus comatus	shaggy mane
Coprinus micaceus (Fig. 108)	early inky mushroom
Fistulina hepatica	beafsteak mushroom
Hydnum caputursi	bears head
Hydnum corralloides	coral fungus
Hypholoma perplexum	red hypholoma
Lactarius deliciosus	milky mushroom*
Lepiota procera	parasol mushroom
Marasmius oreades	fairy ring
Morchella esculenta (Fig. 109)	morel mushroom
Pleurotus ostreatus	oyster mushroom
Pleurotus ulmarius	elm mushroom
Pluteus cervinus	pluteus
Polyporus sulphureus	sulphur mushroom
Russula virescens	green russula
Steccherinum	see Hydnum above
Strobilomyces strobilaceus	pine cone mushroom

Some general rules for beginners on what to avoid when gathering mushrooms are (1) avoid any species you do not know to be edible (2) avoid any mushrooms beginning to show age (3)

---

*Many milky mushrooms are poisonous and even though this specimen is edible one should be cautious of any which oozes a milky juice.

avoid all mushrooms in the button stage (4) avoid all mushrooms with a scaly bulb at the base of the stem (5) avoid all mushrooms with small pores under the cap (6) avoid woodland mushrooms with a bright red cap and white gills below (7) avoid yellow orange mushrooms in late summer growing at the base of stumps, and (8) avoid any mushroom with white milky juice.

LICHENS

ICELAND MOSS   *Cetraria islandica*

This is a tufted lichen, it appears as olive drab mats with red splotches. Funnel shaped tufts rise and divide at their summits from the mats. It is a ground plant which is highly nutritious. If it appears to be bitter then a second boiling is in order.

ROCK TRIPE   *Umbilicaria pustulata*   **Figure 110**

This is a lichen which grows on boulders and jutting rocks usually in highland regions. It appears as rubbery plates, gray to greenish in color above and tan below. The upper surface on some species appears to have bubbles or blisters on it. These can be boiled slowly for about an hour and served as soup. For real zest throw in a few wild onion bulbs.

Fig. 110   Rock Tripe

More on Mushrooms and *The Foolproof Four*

When I was eight years old and skipping second grade on a warm September day I rolled under a barbed wire fence and roamed through a cow field. Before I reached the other side I found a big patch of meadow mushrooms and took off my hat and loaded it with the mushrooms. My mother was familiar with mushrooms and she immediately made me a lunch of scrambled eggs and mushrooms. It was a significant moment in my life because it set me on a hobby that consumed much of my time for the rest of my life. This event was near the end of the Great Depression and at that age I realized there was free food out there for the taking. I am eighty nine years old at this writing and still look for the meadow mushroom, as well as their cousins..

Mushrooms are an interesting facet of our wild foods offerings and millions of people all over the world go searching for them. You can too, but if you are new to the pursuit you should go with someone who is experienced with mushrooms. You can learn much from books and articles on the subject, but you are at risk if you only rely on books on the subject.

Just after the war in Vietnam the United States permitted our compatriots of that country whose lives were in jeopardy to immigrate to our country. A group of four Vietnamese went mushroom hunting in the forests near Olympia, Washington. They gathered mushrooms that looked like the ones they ate back home, but alas, they had gathered the "Death Angel" which was similar to an edible species of their home country. They all died. The Death Angel is completely white, has a bulbous root and a small curtain around its stem. Its toxin sets up a ping-pong battle between the liver and kidneys and the toxins cannot leave the body.

On one of my field excursions I ran across Maria, an elderly neighbor lady with a basket of mushrooms on her arm. I peeked into her basket and examined them and gave my approval. She had a couple quarters in the bottom of her basket and assured me they had not turned black. That was her method of identifying poisonous mushrooms, which was not very trustworthy and not recommended. Besides, you can't get a silver quarter anymore.

There are at least thirty edible mushrooms growing in the spring, summer, and autumn woods. Some of the most enjoyable are "stumpies" or the little inky mushrooms related to the "shaggy mane" which will grow on your lawn if you don't mow it. These grow at the base of trees, especially the stumps of harvested trees.

All mushrooms have local names and scientists frown on the use of local names when seriously discussing mushrooms, or anything else for that matter.

In the world of mushroom hunting there are four mushrooms known as the "**Foolproof Four**" since they do not look like any other species. Maybe not so. Read on.

The first of the "foolproof four" is the **puffball**. How can you make a mistake here? Well sir, you can harvest a small round mushroom that resembles a puffball but hasn't fully opened up yet. Also, there is a mushroom locally known in our lake region as "the pigskin mushroom" which looks like a ball and it is to be avoided.

The second of the group is "**chicken of the woods**" that grows at the base of trees. This is a truly enjoyable treat when properly cooked. You must be aware of the environment when harvesting the chicken-of-the-woods. If it grows on conifers then it will probably make you ill if you consume it. Harvest the chicken in deciduous areas.

The third easy to identify mushroom is the **morel** whose skin looks like a sci-fi monster, but looks are deceiving and this is probably the most sought after mushroom by enthusiasts. I have found them along bike trails, in brushy meadows, and cemeteries. People actually offered me money to tell them where they can find them. There are also mushrooms called "false morel." Need I say more.

The fourth in this category is the Chanterelle, an orange mushroom that grows in woodlands and at the border of woodlands., There is a confusing cousin of the Chanterelle. It's name is the Jack-O-Lantern mushroom. It won't kill you, but it certainly won't please your innards if you eat it.

Wild mushrooms are fun, but before you start to mess with them you should forage with someone who has successfully done so and lived to tell the tale. There are mushroom clubs near every large city and they should be consulted if there is one near you. Never eat anything from the wild unless you are certain that you recognize it and know it to be edible.

A giant puffball with its skin beginning to crack.

A chanterelle mushroom with its vase shape.

A pair of morel mushrooms.

Chicken-of-the-woods on the base of a deciduous tree.

Photo album of people and wild plants

Euell Gibbons and John Tomikel at North Bend State Park, West Virginia, September 1973. The Gibbons book, *Stalking the Wild Asparagus* was just beginning to enjoy national attention at this time.

Figure 2: The late Euell Gibbons, center, and John Tomikel, right, lead a discussion of edible wild plants at a seminar at North Bend State Park, West Virginia.

Photo by Bonnie Henderson September 1975. Euell Gibbons name had become a household word when this photo was taken. Euell Gibbons died a few months after this meeting took place.

The back cover of the first printing of Edible Wild Plants of Eastern United States and Canada. We could only find a worn copy.

In his first book on edible wild plants Dr. Tomikel stated that it was not written as a survival manual. This work carries along that same theme and so such plants as skunk cabbage and jack in the pulpit which may have edible parts are eliminated from this volume. "It is a disservice to the reader to occupy time with them."

The purpose of this work is to provide a usuable illustrated reference which is inexpensive to the wild plant hobbyist. Dr. Tomikel considers the gathering and preparation of wild plants a hobby rather than a necessity. Even though some of his friends consider eating wild plants a "mystical experience" the author refrains from such inference.

The author serves up a wild stew at an outdoor seminar.

Photo By Monongahela
Daily Herald

Edeline Wood

Edeline Wood, President of the National Wild Foods Association and originator of Nature Wonder Weekend. The National Wild Foods Association inducts one natural foods person into its Hall of Fame each year. Euell Gibbons was the first inductee in the twentieth century and JohnTomikel was the last inductee in that era.

Lichen – rock tripe - page 93

Tansy – an old herbal remedy – page 84

Solomon's Seal root – pages 65 and 82

Marsh Marigold – do not eat it raw – page 72

Broad Leaf Dock – all docks are edible when cooked page 63

Purslane – a premier salad green – portulaca – page 79

Wild grapes – pages 36 and 37
eat raw, make wine, make jelly

Gooseberry - some have prickles on them – page 37

Sunflower along a railroad track   page 84

John Tomikel

Photo of the author taken at a wild foods conference in 1984.
He was 56 years old at the time.

Wild parsnip. Notice the dill-head. When we were kids these grew along the railroad tracks and we ate our fill of the roots. Our mothers probably wondered why we weren't hungry at supper.

We used to hollow out the stems of elderberry shoots and use the unripe fruit of the wild black cherry tree for ammunition. My first attempt at making elderberry wine ended in three gallons of vinegar that no one wanted to use.

Pigweed? Bad name. Green Amaranth and Redroot are more desirable. My friend Ron Boone mixed the boiled leaves with a can of mushroom soup and we had a royal feast along with acorn bread.

Staghorn sumac. Once my son Matthew learned to make sumac tea he did a lot of experimenting with it and came up with many delicious variations.

INDEX

Warning: Caution: Some road and railroad right-of-ways are sprayed with weed killer. Avoid any area that appears to be in poor health.

Weeds are simply plants that appear out-of-place